The Career Catapult

Shake Up the Status

Quo and Boost Your

Professional Trajectory

Roopa Unnikrishnan

CAREER PRESS

The Career Press, Inc.
Wayne, NJ

CAREER CATAPULT
EDITED BY ROGER SHEETY
TYPESET BY PERFECTYPE, NASHVILLE, TENNESEE
Cover design by Jonathan Bush Design
Cover image by Sergey Nivens/shutterstock
Paper images by Picsfive/shutterstock
Printed in the U.S.A.

To order this title, please call toll-free 1-800-CAREER-1 (NJ and Canada: 201-848-0310) to order using VISA or MasterCard, or for further information on books from Career Press.

The Career Press, Inc.
12 Parish Drive
Wayne, NJ 07470
www.careerpress.com
www.newpagebooks.com

Library of Congress Cataloging-in-Publication Data

CIP Data Available Upon Request.

Dedicated to

My father, whose vision and work ethic is, and always will be, a key motivator.

My mother, whose steel backbone and determination is part of my core.

Sree, Durga, and Krishna who surround me every day with sheer joy.

Jalal uncle, who taught me the special magic of the shooting sport.

TP and Lekha who have been like an added set of parents to me.

My siblings, who taught me to keep my chin up, always.

And a special thanks to the global community of TiE (The Indus Entrepreneurs), Ray and Steph, who supported my research efforts immensely

CONTENTS

INTRODUCTION

The Jolt That Set Me Free

We live in an evolving economic environment, one where job security and certainty for the future are a distant memory. The old rules for navigating the turbulent waters of employment don't apply anymore. In the face of these changes, it's easy to become fearful and discouraged. In *The Career Catapult*, through my experience as an innovation and career consultant, I give passionate individuals— regardless of their current position in the job hierarchy—a way to gaze into this uncertain future and shape it to their advantage.

Using the skills and knowledge gained from working with Fortune 500 companies toward success, I look forward to walking you through a doable and innovative five-step plan to achieve your goals in business and find the fulfillment and sense of adventure that everyone truly desires at their core.

This book may challenge your preconceived notions of success and guide you toward defining "achievement" for yourself, equipping you to seize the endless opportunities to make that success a reality in your own life. People who will find *The Career Catapult* essential for career growth are those who are wondering whether they're in the right job, in the right organization, or in the right industry. They worry that their true purpose is calling them, but they just can't hear it. Or perhaps they aren't entirely satisfied with their job, the pay, or their performance. These are the people who likely believed they would achieve something way bigger than mere compliant satisfaction. With *The Career Catapult* they still can.

When someone's career trajectory flatlines, then it's time for a disruption. Using the same disciplines that innovative companies use to achieve high-level success, this five-discipline plan for personal success guides readers to disrupt the status quo and make the leap toward true satisfaction in business and life. I call one of the key elements "bottling serendipity," because there are opportunities constantly presenting themselves—sometimes as obstacles, sometimes as weak signals, and sometimes as trends—that *The Career Catapult* thoughtfully grabs a hold of to drive change in people's lives and careers.

A few years ago, I set out to frame my own sense of self—what drives me, and hence, what drives my actions? Here is the story of my personal journey, which helped lead me to sharing these insights with you.

You'd think I'd be the last person to write about serendipity.

I was 13 when I first contemplated the end of life as I'd known it, the youngest child in a quintessentially striving, middle-class Indian family: three children, a stay-at-home mother, and a father serving as an officer in the highly respected Indian police. Then one day, he was no longer reachable. My father's disappearance unleashed a combination of political and professional conflicts that hit our family. It rocked me to my core. Nothing had ruffled the calm surface of my life until a sunny Friday morning in 1987, when we were turfed out of our flat—the physical manifestation of having been jolted out of our life, out of comfort, out of certainty, out of the future we had expected, and into a very dark unknown. Although my father was back with us within the year, in the eyes of society, we were condemned. With these circumstances and the questions they raised came a black hole of issues that had to be considered and confronted.

As a sheltered 13-year-old, I could in no way understand what had happened to cause our change in circumstances, but I quickly comprehended the nosedive into toxicity from what had been a comfortably elite perch. I saw clearly that I could either curl inward and wait for the bad stuff to go away, or find a way to do precisely the opposite. That was the clarifying part about the jolt.

Curling inward seemed a deadening choice; I went the opposite way. I had earlier shown a talent, encouraged by my father, for rifle shooting. With the support of my mother with her spine of steel, my uncle, and my exceptionally kind shooting coach, I entered competitions—public derision and hostility be damned. Putting myself out there like that was my way of clearing away the fear and embarrassment and asserting instead, "This is me; I am here. I will disrupt everything you think you know about me!" I decided to snatch victory from the fangs of dishonor. This was the cleansing part of the jolt.

———

"Learn from the last shot and keep going." That is how my shooting coach always put it, and it is what the sport teaches. Olympic-style shooting competitions had you shooting 60 shots in about as much time—an hour and 15 minutes. The goal was to shoot right through the center of the target—the 10 ring—aim, breath, account for wind and other factors, squeeze the trigger, follow through, and then look through the telescope to see where the shot landed. Get too excited by a 10 and you risk raising your heart rate and messing up the next shot; get too dismayed by a bad shot and you don't focus on the next shot. This is yogic non-attachment at its best!

I began to win competitions—lots of them. Among other victories, I was named India's 1999 Arjuna Award winner for shooting (India's hall of fame for all sports in India) and in 1998 I brought home the gold medal and record in the Commonwealth Games. It was gratifying indeed to make my own headlines—"Roopa Wins Gold!"—and to realize I had the skills and power to create my own future. You take what you can from the last shot, set up the next, assess what's before you, and keep going. That's the liberating part of the jolt.

Thanks to my father's keen eye, we had discovered my sporting gift just a few years ago when I was 11, but this event drove me to the kind of efforts I didn't know I had the capacity for.

What I also learned, however—perhaps because I was so young and so utterly helpless in the face of the jolt to life as I had known it—was just how powerful a force a jolt can be. I vowed to learn how to marshal that power so that I could become the agent of the jolt, not a puppet of it or bystander to it. I would jolt myself to my own purposes and for my own benefit.

That is exactly what I did, and it worked. Rhodes Scholar, senior corporate vice president, managing director, founder of my own consulting firm, and mother of twins—I have enjoyed a catalogue of personal successes that have enriched my life, have done some good in the world, and have had exhilarating experiences. And I did it by learning to *disrupt* myself *forward* repeatedly, whenever needed.

Through the years, I've continued to refine the process as I've moved from jolt to jolt, from one job to another, among different organizations, across oceans and continents, and from country to country and culture to culture. I have crystallized the process into a sequence of five action steps that empowered me to create and execute my own jolts, as needed, and it is this process that I now want to impart to you.

———

Where does all this leave me?

In many ways, my father's jolt—which was my own jolt—had set me free to build exactly the kind of capabilities that get innovators going. I had been freed from any expectations. Nobody expected anything, so I set my own standards and my own goals. I learned that I could and should take risks by trying whatever I could. Then there was my coach who told me to "never let them see me cry." That got me focused and driven.

Later in life, there would be the serendipity of the lazy afternoon when my father had popped open an encyclopedia to show me the entry on Cecil Rhodes. Reading about his colonial expeditions hadn't been fun, but the bit about the Rhodes Scholarships stuck. When all else seemed out of reach—honor, a simple Indian life—I decided to shoot for the difficult targets. That short afternoon read became part of my path forward and onward.

Fourteen years after that fateful day, I found myself in New York. In the intervening years, I had won international medals, been conferred the Indian presidential honor for outstanding sportsmanship, the Arjuna Award, and gone to Oxford as a Rhodes Scholar. The path to that move had been paved by serendipitous meetings, conversation, and effort. Defining my pathway in a new industry, in a new city, and among a whole new peer group was another adventure. Learning to shift from a task-driven mindset to becoming a more collegial and empathetic colleague was key to my own growth. Parlaying a chance cocktail review of the "leaks" in a bank's customer experience (when my experience put me off the bank) to a strategy role in the company, a coffee discussion with an old client about new technologies that resulted in his creating a role around new technology use by the executive leaders of the organization—these were all serendipitous moments that helped me earn my innovation stripes and coaching mastery. In this book, I share some of the lessons that I gathered along the way.

And what of my black holes—the factors that hold me back? I've worked for the longest time to be more empathetic. If anything, my becoming a coach was because I knew I had to learn to work with others' needs, not just their ambitions. Colleagues who knew me 15 years ago will tell you what a shift it's been. It took a lot of friction with peers for me to truly understand that it wasn't about my thinking or my work. It was about my taking the time to engage with the people around me. It's a simple thought, but a tough one for someone who had been so alienated, so early, and for whom the only way forward was work and effort. Fifteen years on, I am a business coach who has taken on the role of helping others find their path, not thinking or working on their behalf. It's taken a while, but it's been so fulfilling!

Jolts stop us in our tracks, but they can also provide the momentum to shift to new paths to success.

So, Is This About Disruption?

Yes, it is—personal disruption. From Schumpeter's theory that free markets are driven by continuous innovation and creative destruction, to Clayton Christensen's use of disruptive innovation as an action plan, disruptions to the status quo—intentional, programmed, and managed—have a long and diverse history. Today, the 21st-century variant of disruption is at work at the very highest and lowest levels within the product and service universe, where corporate strategists unleash new technologies precisely to disrupt the marketplace. The aim is to establish a new market and value network that will unsettle existing value networks till the new technology displaces the previous technology. The marketplace advances—and the company advances—at least until the next disruption. It's also relevant to the individual, to you and me, to be precise.

I'd like to work with you on driving innovation in your personal life. However, disruptive innovation doesn't happen by magic. It isn't limited to just a few companies or cultures, nor is it driven by a "eureka!" moment of sudden inspiration. Innovations that jolt a career, an industry, or a life are achieved by people and companies that have built out a set of disciplines, whether deliberately or by chance, that keep their innovation gene up and running. These disciplines open these people's and companies' eyes and ears to the signals around them, open their minds to their inherent possibilities, and make them unafraid to experiment. That's what drives innovation, and it is a discipline that is well worth amping up in all our lives.

In the personal version of this, the individual needs to jump-start the shift in his or her current perceived value up a notch in the marketplace—shift the marketplace itself to establish a new perception of himself or herself. This will help them move not just the career but also the individual's natural self up and forward, strategically and repeatedly. It's about innovating a life, not just a job. It's also about being open to the possibilities around you. Capture those serendipitous opportunities and insights; don't let them get away. Look deep into what might be appearing before you and then experiment or make something of that opportunity.

The magic lies in making a habit—even a plan—out of these disciplines. There are a small number of disciplines involved in bottling serendipity. We will leverage data from a survey on innovation-oriented behaviors with responses from 300 executives across a broad range of companies and nonprofits. Clear trends and commonalities support the insights and approach shared in the book. Whereas existing innovation surveys either look at organizational dynamics or group behaviors, the survey we designed captures individual and organizational attributes and surfaces correlations between these factors, as well as how the individual's own innovation appetite shifts their perception of the world, their work, and opportunities. This in turn converts to a willingness to act on their own behalf.

Applied to the realities of an individual's work life and turned into the equivalent of a personal career management plan, this approach serves the individual career in the same way a company manages its strategy. Companies do this all the time; they understand who they are, they identify their core competencies, and they acknowledge the gaps in products, markets, and abilities. They then fan out to find ways to address gaps, but in many ways the biggest shifts have come from capturing a great moment or chance encounter. At the heart of acquisitions and new products are those insights that come from a leader making sense of a trend they hadn't seen before.

Being open to this kind of serendipity, as an individual, can be a disruptive shock to the current career trajectory, and yes, it rocks the stability of that career. But it's a quantum advance. As the world shifts around you—with new information and new stakeholders emerging—I will walk you through the disciplines that will prime you to make the best use of the opportunities that present themselves to you and those that you develop. *This* is how you bottle serendipity.

The Five Disciplines

Leaping into a revised career trajectory requires quick, sudden, and purposeful movement. Each of the five disciplines builds upon the other, moving individuals along the fast track toward success and fulfillment. Each action reframes how readers look at their business lives within a fluctuating context. Culminating with Discipline 5, readers get the big shift they've been working toward and achieve maximum velocity toward their ideal career goals.

- **Discipline 1: Dig Deep to Soar!**
  Examine your skills and resources to accurately assess your marketplace value as well as your attitude toward what constitutes success and how growth is measured.
- **Discipline 2: Stalk Innovations and Trends.** Explore the context in which you can offer your value by tracking market innovations and emerging trends, and deciphering how they apply to you in the workforce.
- **Discipline 3: Your Network on Jolt!** Use your assets, including networks that can drive significant value, to test and build upon what you've discovered as you looked both inward and outward.
- **Discipline 4: Prototype the Possibilities.** Start by challenging everything you've learned from digging deep and stalking trends and focus only on what has

the potential to lead to success and fulfillment. Free yourself to imagine. Visualize the full array of possibilities and test-drive them. Find ways to don the mantle of the new role—volunteer, experiment with a start-up, join a professional group—and see how this new space might work out for you.

- **Discipline 5: Go Extreme!** Is your desired future achievable? Yes—then take that confident leap into your future.

How to Read This Book for Greatest Impact

The impetus for my writing this book came from the multiple discussions I had with colleagues who struggled with the constraints of their roles, and with the prospect of being "stuck," as well as my coaching sessions with clients who felt left behind after years of contributing to the goals of corporations. It is also an homage to the intrepid entrepreneurs and investors who put their effort and money where their mouth is.

In the following chapters, I will share vignettes that describe composite characters. In most cases, the gender and industry of the composite characters are fictitious, but the circumstances and tenure of the composite tends to reflect a common characteristic of real coaching clients I have worked with. I also share stories of real innovators and I thank them for letting me share their stories. In such cases, I have highlighted where they are real-life characters.

Throughout the various chapters of *The Career Catapult*, "Checkpoints" present intriguing research findings, and "Take Action" sections give readers the opportunity to relate the information provided to their own circumstances and clearly establish what steps to take at each interval. I also use the term "jolt" to represent opportunities or obstacles that cause shifts in thinking.

You'll also find worksheets that can guide you through the five disciplines. You can download these worksheets at *http://TheCareerCatapult.com*. Use these worksheets as an active guide to your personal career catapult.

In addition to my in-depth experience with clients and coaches, I have had the opportunity to interview innovators across the globe and I will draw from a survey of 300 entrepreneurs, business people, and a control group of non-corporate participants. This will allow us to contrast learnings between those who identify themselves as innovators, execution-oriented individuals, and other categories.

A fascinating set of observed patterns have fed this book, and I suggest you have a pencil handy to work on some of the exercises I provide in each of the chapters.

CHAPTER 1

Why a Career Catapult? Design Your Own Destiny

This isn't a book about luck; it's a book about making the most of what the world throws at you.

There are circumstances in life that only a shock can free you from: the relationship that hasn't been going anywhere for far too long; the 20 extra pounds you put on when you quit smoking five years ago; the half-finished manuscript of your novel stuffed into the desk drawer; your dream of exotic travel stuffed into the *other* desk drawer. When good intentions, willpower, or reminding yourself that "life is short" aren't enough to thrust you out of whatever stagnation or complacency you're in, you need a jolt.

A jolt stops you in your tracks, turns you around, and pushes you in another direction, unnerving though it may be. It catapults you from where you are to some other place. A jolt is qualitatively different from the sort of cool, considered modifications through which most of us fine-tune our lives. A jolt isn't about editing and revising; it's about the kind of transformation that clarifies, cleanses, and liberates.

An educated guess here, but if you're reading this book, one element of your life that surely needs to be jolted is your career. That's why you picked up this book. Because even if your career looks good on paper, even if it feels good from day to day, you sense that your work life needs to advance, change places, or refocus.

Maybe you're caught in the "golden prison career" syndrome: bored to the point of numbness, but shackled by the paycheck and bonuses. Or maybe your career is humming along very nicely indeed—so nicely that you can succeed at it with one hand tied behind your back, and certainly without ever having to stretch your brain.

Maybe, like so many of your contemporaries, you are wondering whether you're really in the right job, in the right organization, or in the right industry. You worry that your true purpose is calling you, but you just can't hear it.

Or it could be that you're entirely satisfied with your job, the pay, and your performance. But, hey, weren't you the person who was going to live life flat out, live it large, and achieve something way bigger than mere satisfaction?

Whatever the case may be, you need a career jolt.

I've seen careers jolted every which way: I've seen an ER doctor jolted into a social entrepreneur saving lives in Africa; a white-shoed lawyer jolted into a sandal-wearing Silicon Valley entrepreneur. The jolts were deliberate—and I helped make them happen.

We think of jolts as happening *to* us. They're a surprise—sometimes a shock. We understand them only in retrospect. But what if you could control the jolt, just as the ER doctor, the lawyer, and the assembly line worker did? What if you could cause it to happen, program its content ahead of time, and command it? Couldn't you then shape the transformation it produces, as they did? Couldn't you ready yourself for a new love, lose the weight, finish the novel, free yourself of those silken shackles, and change jobs, careers, or lifestyles and head for the life you imagine? You could, and you can. That's what this book is about.

For the most part, the average career-management guide today reads like a warrior's manual. It tells you how to draw up your battle plan, deploy your forces, and take that hill. It trains you to go out and engage "the enemy"—the enemy in this case being the job market, the organization you want to work for, or the dream job you want to define for yourself.

Reality is actually a lot more complex, and it makes little sense to be at war with it. Taking the hill is rarely enough; the hill is only a stopping point between where you start and where you want to finish. Reality is about the finish, and it is about the journey toward it, day after day, as you grow into the person you want to be and can be.

Creating the disruptions that will take you forward and upward on that advance, therefore, begins with digging deep to understand who you are and who you can be. It requires knowing the context in which you advance—the economic environment and the business trends and the resources that you can draw upon. But, above all, creating the jolt is an act of the imagination and intellect, and it must be challenged and tested against the facts of reality. That is why each chapter provides worksheets that help you quantify your progress through each action step, enabling you to do the hands-on scrutiny and analysis that is so essential to the process.

Your work shapes so much of your life in so many ways, and if you have reached the point where you're wondering whether it is worth it, you need to find out if it is. If it isn't, jolt yourself into a career that is.

Are you ready? Let's begin.

———

Now, let me introduce you to Lindsay (a composite of two clients), a successful professional by any measure. The head of the digital team at a well-known financial behemoth, she fell into, rather than aimed for, this field, but is grateful for the results. It was her parents who had urged her to focus on technology in college, and it was a bank that had recruited her after graduation to run a small technical marketing project. A bit more than a decade later, Lindsay leads the holding company's effort to bring new tools and Web platforms to marketing efforts, does it successfully, and is amply rewarded—at least financially.

But the truth is that Lindsay, now in her mid-30s, feels that she has sleepwalked her way through her career and has decided she doesn't want to sleep-walk through her future. When she examines her own capabilities, she sees a woman who can take ownership of an initiative and guide it through to successful completion—a marketable value, especially in conjunction with her technical skills. But it's a value she has thus far "sold" to an industry she cares little about in return for financial compensation that buys her escapes from the career, namely, global travel to satisfy her love of history and her passion for learning about and cooking the great cuisines of the world.

Wouldn't it be wonderful, Lindsay thinks as she checks the contents of her briefcase and sets forth for yet another day at the office, if the remaining decades of my work life could somehow serve what I love while taking advantage of what I am good at?

It would, and it can. But to make it happen, Lindsay must jolt her career out of its complacency—jolt it forward to a career that rewards her with meaning as well as money, and jolt it upward to a level of work that engages her ardor, not just her sense of obligation. To do that, she will have to look to the very same strategy of innovation that has jolted new industries into being and reinvented the 21st-century global economy— and she will have to pointedly disrupt her own career trajectory.

Disrupt?

Yes, disrupt.

As I mentioned, this disruption is not about destruction; it's about creating new value. Both the marketplace and the company advance until the next disruption.

To carry this out on a personal level, the individual unleashes not a new technology, per se, but a thoughtfully programmed revamping of his or her professional profile, capabilities, and circumstances.

The intention, however, is the same as that of the corporate strategist: to displace the individual's previous perceived value and, equally important, to do it ahead of the curve so as not to be disrupted out of relevance by the fast-paced changes happening around us at all times.

Applied to one's work life and turned into a personal career-management plan, the jolt thus serves the individual's career in the same way. Yes, it's a disruptive shock to the current career trajectory, and yes, it rocks the stability of that career, but it does so by advancing it to a new plane. That is why jolting a career is something that can and should be done repeatedly; the aim is to disrupt and advance, again and again—as often as needed to move the career forward and upward. With each jolt, the individual refines his or her capabilities, personal brand, and mental approach to work, life, and career anew.

That's exactly what Lindsay did. You have sensed that you need to do the same; it's why you're reading this book. But a disruption!—with the exclamation point almost inherent to it—sounds so radical. Isn't it fair to ask, "Is now the time?"

Checkpoints: Survey Insights

Aside from my personal observations, this book was inspired by client work where I had found consistent themes among technical and business innovators, as well as themes that emerged from my experience coaching senior executives.

In developing original research for this book, I ran an innovation survey among a group of more than 300 business professionals, including CEOs, business owners and entrepreneurs, founders of nonprofits, consultants, and even folks who work in many traditional corporate functions such as legal, sales, operations, finance, and accounting. We asked them for their thoughts on innovation, the practices they see in their own organizations, whether they see themselves as innovators, and how their upbringings, mentors, education, and companies influenced their own innovative and creative abilities. The results were insightful and not different from what I've seen in my years of work.

One key conclusion is that innovation is not a stroke of luck or a natural gift; rather, it is an ongoing discipline that people and companies pursue. Instead of hoping for a "eureka!"

moment, the vast majority (70 percent) of respondents in our survey said that their companies would continuously scan the environment to capture new ideas. Similarly, our survey showed that the majority (53 percent) of people who considered their work role to be new idea generation would develop their innovation capabilities through *focused practice*. Specifically, these individuals would constantly engage with books, magazines, newspapers, conferences, workshops, courses, podcasts, and so on.

Another key finding is that the definition of innovation among our business professionals is not just one thing; it is many things. Twenty-three percent of respondents believed innovation was about new products and services; 16 percent believed innovation is about new ways of sharing information and goods; 10 percent believed it was about changing existing products and services; and 51 percent believed it was a puzzle of two or more of the aforementioned pieces. From this, we can see that innovation does not necessarily have to be just any one product or service offering. Instead, it can be a combination of several concepts and ongoing, rather than a single object or event.

Among our total sample, we also wanted to look at specific subgroups and see what unique characteristics can be uncovered within these groups. As the initial trigger for innovation is often new ideas, we looked at a group of respondents whose primary role in innovation was new idea generation (incidentally, this group also happened to rate themselves highly on intellectual curiosity, perseverance, and open-mindedness). Among this group, we found that they more often (66 percent) see their role in innovation as occurring with others—either in teams at work or with associates outside of the workplace—rather than by themselves. Moreover, they have frequent and consistent contact with a large network (59 percent had networks with more than 50 people).

The key takeaways that I would glean are:

- Innovation is not an innate characteristic that only a select few people are born with. It is a skill that can be practiced, developed, and harnessed through continuous learning.
- Innovation is complex and ongoing; it does not have to be just about one new

thing. It can be many things either at one point or throughout a period of time.

- Innovators themselves do not sit in a vacuum waiting for inspiration to strike. They study and contemplate in search of new insights in the world, and they collaborate and network with others to further their ideas.

Career Planning in a Changing World

Look around you. The global business landscape is going through a roller-coaster ride of gyrations, and it is growing increasingly vicious. Talented people—the kind of professionals you would assume to be layoff-proof—have found themselves labeled "redundant" or unnecessary not just once, but repeatedly, as the old, "standard" jobs simply disappear. Meanwhile, those jobs that remain have become more demanding in the extreme: longer hours, more intense work, and roles that cross over and often blur professional, social, and personal spheres.

We understand that we are in the midst of an unprecedented economic transition, and when we look at that transition from the point of view of the individual's work life, we see that the old rules simply don't apply anymore. Yes, there was a time when "career planning" meant thinking in terms of a two-axis matrix—a timeline on one axis and levels of hierarchical advancement on the other—then setting goals for climbing the ladder in five- or 10-year segments. That simply doesn't work today.

For one thing, there are fewer rigid hierarchies. Although the Fortune 500 accounted for

Career Paths Evolve

From Linear To Multi-Dimensional
Opportunities and Growth

20 percent of employment in the United States in 1970, their share had dropped to 8.5 percent by 1996, and ongoing productivity gains continue to shrink their workforce size. Most jobs—and not just in the United States—reside in smaller firms, which have typically been the incubators of economic growth and job creation. This reality has become particularly conspicuous in today's innovation economy of extra-establishment and sometimes anti-establishment start-ups.

Equally determinative, *how* one succeeds has also changed. In the more growth-oriented sections of today's economy, success comes not to those who wait, but to those who are proactive about what is needed, even if it is not wanted *right now.* Success comes to those who move, engage, network, see, and communicate the possibilities, and get things done.

There's an upside to all this confusing flux, and this is where the idea of the jolt earns its spurs: now more than ever, every individual in search of a life's work has the chance fully to realize his or her inherent talent in pursuit of a unique mission aimed at the twin goals of financial success and personal fulfillment. Clearly, if you are going to seize that chance and keep it fresh, you need to rethink—even redefine—the entire process of career planning.

Staying put is not an option; if you stand still while others move forward, you will soon be left behind. So *sustaining* a career won't cut it. That is why the aim instead is to *disrupt* your work style and career in such a way as to burst your opportunities open—to shift yourself up and ahead to new capabilities that enrich your profile, to open new markets, to a change in direction for growth.

Equally, that's why disruptive innovation must become an action plan as well as a watchword. We've seen the concept applied to education, healthcare, government, journalism, and, of course, business strategy. The jolt puts it to work for the individual career, whether you are just setting out, are ready to change the career you have, or want to turbo-charge your progress.

So the answer to "Is now the time?" is that there has never been a better time to reach out and grab the work, life and career goals you want—and to do so with a disruption!

CHAPTER 2

Discipline #1: Dig Deep to Soar!

When Lindsay came to me for consulting assistance on her career, her first question was "Where do I start?" I gave her a simple answer: her starting point is herself. I give you the exact same answer: "Start with you."

After all, if what you're after is a career and life that rewards you with meaning and engages your ardor, you need to figure out what you mean by those terms. What is the meaning you seek as a reward in your work life, and what are the kinds of activities or circumstances that engage your ardor in other spheres of life? In short, what you have to determine is what Lindsay had to determine— what motivated her, what she wanted out of her life, and how her career could advance and support what she wanted out of her life.

These are profound questions, and Lindsay had to dig deep to answer them. So will you.

DIG DEEP TO SOAR!

As I talked to and surveyed innovators across a series of cutting edge companies, a few core capabilities and mindsets came to the fore. Those capabilities are the goal posts for the discipline of digging deep. Understand which of those capabilities you *have* built with time, and if not, understand what prevented you from honing them. We'll discuss ways by which you can confront those truths and begin working on them. You may never fully get to 100 percent, but who does? It's about knowing what it takes, understanding what it might look like for you, and then beginning the "muscle-building" effort—the exercises that will help you evolve yourself and your mindset.

Three Spheres of Yourself

Ancient philosophies have multiple weighty tomes to offer you about self-knowledge. Ironically, I found it is the business world that offers a workable model for digging deep into the self and answering these questions honestly and straightforwardly. Any business organization ready for a change goes through precisely such a process. Whether its projected change is to grow, expand, rebrand, or even contract, the organization takes time to assess exactly what it is changing *from* and to ensure it has the wherewithal to make the change it seeks. It examines its core competencies, analyzes its P&L (profit and loss) statement, and evaluates its employee base and leadership profile. This is neither a simple nor a short process, and it typically sets in motion a number of transforming actions that demand considerable effort from employees across the organization. But such organizational self-awareness is the essential starting-point for any evolutionary change.

The individual's equivalent of an organizational self-assessment is not so different. When organizations catalogue their core competencies, they're looking at their strengths, what they're good at. When they analyze profit and loss, they're probing for weaknesses. When they check out the people who do the work and the folks who lead them, they're trying to understand what really drives the place. You will do the same, assessing yourself in three spheres to create your self-awareness map: core capabilities, black holes, and motivating passions.

Checkpoint: Survey Insights

In our survey of 300 professionals, the majority (71 percent) of respondents who play a key role in generating new ideas deliberately take time to personally reflect on their strengths, capabilities, and gaps at least once a month.

Self-awareness is a key component to career success and most career innovators strive to evaluate and improve. When was the last time you

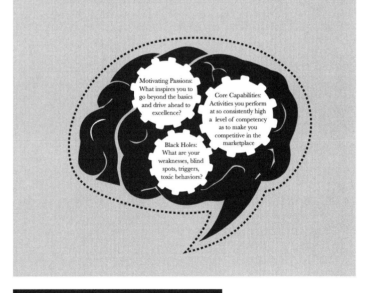

The Three Spheres Of Yourself

dug deep and did a full assessment of your capabilities, skills, and black holes?

Core Capabilities

For a company, core capabilities are those business activities it performs so well that the activities may be said to be critical to its competitive position in the marketplace. It's the same for you. Your core capabilities are those functions or tasks you do at so consistently high a level of competency that they make you competitive in the marketplace. In market terms, they may be said to define you. With Lindsay, for example, her core capability was clearly her competence in managing a project or function of any size, configuration, and purpose— that is, if you want to be sure it gets done, put Lindsay in charge, no matter how complicated it is and especially if it's critical to your success.

Black Holes

Organizations call them "weaknesses;" I think of them as black holes—the activities, functions, or challenges you just disappear into without a trace.

These are your blind spots, the toxic behaviors you sometimes resort to, the things that trigger your worst qualities, the actions or inactions that hold you back, and yes, the things you're just not very good at. For Lindsay, it was micromanagement—she needed to own all the moving pieces and know exactly when each decision got made. It was impossible for her to free herself up to look upward and engage with her leaders in more forward-looking possibilities while she kept busying herself with operational trouble-shooting (which she could have left to her team).

Motivating Passions

It was Daniel Pink, in his 2011 book, *Drive*, who argued that money and other external rewards do not ignite high performance and satisfaction nearly as much as does the deeply human need to direct our own lives, to learn and create new things, and to do better by ourselves and our world. Pink put into words what most of us intuit. In fact, some studies have found that nonmonetary compensation designed and delivered with thought and care can have more than double the return on financial incentives.[1] This would seem to be mathematical confirmation that the real motivating passion is within us and that it is measurable in external material terms as well as in internal satisfaction. It's a matter of knowing what the motivating passions are that really drive you. In Lindsay's case, of course, her motivating passions were her love of travel and diverse cuisines.

How will you assess these three essential spheres? Two perspectives are required. First, you need to know how others see you—what they regard as your strengths and weaknesses, what they believe drives your actions. At the same time, you need to know how you see yourself. Then you need to put the two together to see where the discrepancies are and what opportunities for change these discrepancies might suggest. How is all that to happen?

How Others See You

The two components of determining how others perceive you are the people you ask and the kinds of assessments you elicit from them. Clearly, you want to reach out to a diverse and challenging group of people who will give you the broadest and deepest understanding of how you are perceived. As you engage your interviewees in your discussions, map their responses to see how they perceive you.

Consider the following potential interviewee types:

Your supervisor or senior leaders who have had the opportunity to work with you or watch you in action: Because these are people who have a vision for the organization or team, they can help you get a sense of how you are perceived from a top-down perspective, especially around whether you get things done and whether you have the skills and mentality ("fit") that align with the company culture.

Peers with whom you have collaborated or with whom you need to spend time for work-related issues: Peers tend to engage with you with greater clarity, without the authority you wield over junior colleagues or the distance and formality that separates you from senior executives. Peers have the access and mindset to watch and judge your collaborative nature and your approach to solving problems. They often also have similar levels of access to information, so they can judge whether you're savvy or not about the company and industry.

Team members are those who support you or work on projects you manage. Team members can be very clear on talent and management issues: How have you helped them grow, have you supported their aspirations, have you helped them deliver their best results, and have you managed multiple priorities to make their work manageable?

Influencers are those who understand the company culture and know about your work and impact. This is a group that can help you understand your informal impact on the organization: Are you seen as a good player, as someone who strengthens the company by bringing their best to work?

Take Action: Plan Your Feedback Gathering

Who on your list will be open to a full-fledged, candid 360-degree interview in which you go through a list of questions and take time to capture the information as your interviewee speaks? There may be political or unsaid issues to consider. If you are in a feedback-friendly environment, just asking for a meeting where you are looking for feedback might work. If yours is an organization less inclined to such candor, consider setting up your interview as a discussion on how you can focus your personal development efforts. You might say you are creating a professional plan for yourself, and because you value their insights, could they share their reflections in a few key areas?

However you structure each interview, know ahead of time what you are trying to learn from it. You will no doubt want to add subject matters relevant to your organization and certainly to your individual situation, but here is a guide to general areas you might probe. It is based on the ways innovators who have made changes in their lives and careers have differentiated themselves.

Focus: What Are You Trying to Understand?

- **General reflections on work products and working style:** How have things worked? What could have been done differently? What can you do more or less of? What should you stop doing?
- **Insights on your capabilities and black holes:**
  - Business owner risk appetite: Based on your work together, how would

they describe your approach to the company and the work you do together? For example, when have they found your understanding and advocacy for the company helpful? Would they describe you as externally focused? If so, what kind of things do you talk about or understand best? Where have your thoughts on customers and other stakeholders (such as buyers and regulators) been helpful?

- Personal accountability: Do you thrive on increasing levels of responsibility, and do you evidence this by taking actions to move the business forward, even when decisions are shared or ambiguous?
- Are you a talent magnet? What do you do that naturally attracts new talent in the external marketplace? What can you do to build the kind of stature and influence inside the organization that make people want to work with or for you?

- Your innovation orientation: Do you regularly challenge conventional solutions, approaches, and methodologies to constructively surface transformational opportunities for research or business actions? Have there been times when you have shown you are open to developing creative approaches to processes and practices, products and solutions, services, business models, and strategies as things shift?
- Decision-making: When they have a tough decision to make, would they consider having you make the decision? Why? How would they describe you: neutral expert, thoughtful strategist, brainstorm partner, or something else?
- Openness: Are you seen as reflective or open to insights? Do you actively seek feedback? How would they describe your impact on them and their work? Can they share any examples of when you have acted as a role model in dealing with difficult ethical issues or hard to solve problems?

Make sure to start by grounding the discussions in real work and framing your questions as much as possible in a specific project, process, or work output you have "shared" with the person you're interviewing. How had things worked? What could have been done differently? What can you do more or less of? What should you stop doing?

Lindsay called the process her "listening tour." She made a list of coworkers, team members, people who reported to her, and people she reported to. With some, she literally conducted explicit interviews; in other cases, she probed during routine one-on-one meetings to get a sense of how her colleagues saw her.

The results constituted a self-discovery that wasn't totally pleasant. Lindsay learned that although she was respected for her ability to get things done and for her focus on results (good capabilities to possess), her peers saw her as somewhat untrustworthy—"two-faced," one of them said—whereas her team members did not feel confident that she had their backs.

It was hard to hear. Lindsay felt blindsided. She hadn't expected those impressions and, dismayed, she was ready to give up the entire self-assessment effort. But I reminded her that this was precisely what she had set out to learn and, as tough as it might have been to hear, it was good to know.

How did this jibe with her own sense of herself? Lindsay and I sat down to work it out. There were gaps. Lindsay had assumed that focusing on results was what everyone looked to her to do. Bent on "getting it right," she believed she was showing flexibility when she routinely shifted direction and modified the plan. To team members who had to scramble to keep up, this looked like gratuitous equivocation for which they paid the price; to her superiors, it looked like she simply wasn't sure of herself. The perspectives on her abilities could not have been more different.

This was the moment for serious internal reflection. What Lindsay was hearing surprised her and opened her eyes to issues she hadn't really recognized or seen as real problems before. What Lindsay realized was that it was precisely her need to get things right that had always held her within clear lines of action laid down by others—the parents who had guided her studies, the financial industry with its focus on numbers, and the culture of the digital world. She was, in effect, captive within someone else's paradigm of what her life and career should be—not a good location for finding personal or professional fulfillment.

It's time to copy the honesty of her interlocutors in her 360-degree interviews and create her self-awareness map.

The Self-Awareness Map

We humans tend to be less conscious of who we are than we think. For example, in one study, more than 90 percent of drivers thought they were "above average."[2] A mathematical impossibility! This shows limited awareness both of what constitutes above-average driving skill and of self. But when it's time to jolt your life and career out of one stage of development and into another, self-awareness of how you inhabit the three key spheres is an absolute essential.

So here and now, start digging deep, and, with the same honesty you would seek from your interviewees, map the core capabilities that give you the wherewithal to jolt your career, the black holes you'll have to fill or avoid, and the motivating passions that can drive you forward.

Example: Lindsay's Self-Awareness Map

CORE CAPABILITIES	MOTIVATING PASSIONS
Strengths: • Project Management	A. Tourism/Travel
	B. Food/Fine Dining
Capabilities: • Technical Skills	C. History
Overused Skills: • Modifying Plans, Adapting to change	...

BLACK HOLES
(Which behaviors hold you back?)

Communication?
Lack of communication to team members; forgetting to obtain buy-in

Conviction?

Adaptability?
Adjusts too easily to change

Trust?
Seen as two-faced by team members

Control?
Seen as a micromanager

POSSIBILITIES:
(If you could, how would you combine your capabilities and passions?)

• Take on a new job for a company in the travel & entertainment industry
• Develop an app to curate food experiences for ultra-high net worth individuals
• Start a website to feature executive chefs in exotic locations

1. Core Capabilities

Hone in specifically on those core capabilities critical to your competitive position in the marketplace—that is, those core capabilities that make change and innovation possible. You'll want to look especially at the career opportunities starting to show up as you read this book—the opportunities that will define new-world, future-oriented careers—for that is the context in which you will be defining your jolt.

Be aware also that, as the economy has shifted, the traditional definition of what constitutes a "good employee" has changed, even in old-world companies. Organizations that are built on the shifting sands of technology and new consumer trends know full well that it's the individual who drives the kind of change orientation that will help them survive and succeed. You will need to measure up.

Use the following guide to help you get a sense of your capability picture. Use the worksheet to capture insights on the following:

- Technical capabilities: What are the specific skills you've built with time?
- Business owner risk mentality
- Personal accountability
- Talent magnet
- Innovation orientation
- Decision-making and judgment
- Change orientation
- Personal growth and development orientation
- Personal authenticity and maturity

2. Black Holes

We've all seen perfectly capable people stall or fail. Usually, what contributes to the implosion are behaviors they don't see in themselves or behaviors they don't let themselves grow into or out of.

Assessing your own black holes is the hardest part of any self-awareness exercise and for that reason perhaps it is the most important. My decades of work and research confirm to me that there are five areas of behavior and interaction that are particularly prone to danger: communication, conviction, adaptability, trust, and control. How you manage each of these, how you interact with others in each area, and how you are therefore perceived in each constitute a territory ripe for pitfalls from which it can be difficult to extricate yourself. At a minimum, here's a checklist for assessing your personal black holes:

COMMUNICATION

Do you communicate crisply and compellingly? In any organization, no matter its size, doing so is the task—and the responsibility—on which all else rises or falls, succeeds or fails. But what does it mean to communicate crisply and compellingly?

Crispness is essential if you are going to be understood. This means first and foremost to present one single idea at a time and to organize a set of ideas into a logical sequence. Let your listeners take the time they need to absorb and digest one idea before moving ahead with another.

It also means being specific in articulating your ideas. It isn't just that a scattershot approach will lose your audience. It's also because people need to know what to expect if they are to get involved and certainly if they are going to commit to what you have to say. Do you paint a picture with details to help them understand? Do you check to make sure they are following you? Keep in mind that not everyone has your experiences and insights, so they may not get what you are saying, and you should therefore stop and regroup or repeat if necessary.

How crisp a communicator are you?

Equally, communicating compellingly is essential if you are going to get buy-in from the people with whom you're communicating. It begins in speaking the language of the person or people with whom you're communicating. Your listeners need to understand the information you're presenting in a way they can relate to. Certainly, you should weave in anecdotes that illustrate your point—sales teams often rely on this method—but you want to go beyond the anecdotes to data or general principles quickly. In other words, get to the point fast, especially if you are presenting to an investor, strategy leader, or CEO.

Finally, are you aware of emotions you might ignite in both yourself and your audience as you communicate? Might you be challenging your listener's carefully laid out plans? Are you stepping on his or her cherished turf? Or are you stimulating new thinking that may outstrip your own? Being ready to address potential objections and to channel your own feelings as you sense shifts in mood or in the emotional temperature around you is a key component of compelling communication.

How compelling a communicator are you?

CONVICTION

Do you believe in what you're doing or advocating, and can you back your belief with courage?

For example, suppose you consider yourself the true representative of your customer's needs and wants in your company. You believe that by advocating for those wants and needs, you can drive innovation and prevent huge waste as well as gain the gratitude of your customer. How do you back up your advocacy, and how far are you willing to go to do so?

The truth—in both work and life—is that things get done more effectively and more success-fully when you believe in them. When you do, you should be willing to go to bat for your convictions. Are you?

ADAPTABILITY

Just how adaptable are you? In today's business environment, resistance to change is a clear career-ender. Being unwilling to learn new skills and behaviors signals an unwillingness to evolve for the betterment of the organization. This doesn't mean that every change proposed or discussed is a good one. If you believe a suggestion should be rejected, by all means state your reasons for doing so—so long as you are sure you are listening.

Indeed, adaptability is a hard quality to mea-sure in yourself. Check back to your interviews; did any of your feedback indicate you're seen as resistant to change? You might think of yourself as thoughtful and realistic only to realize you're regarded as stodgy and adamant; take another look at yourself to see if there may be merit in that perception.

TRUST

Have your interviews surfaced any suggestions that you may be overly self-absorbed, self-promoting, or, perhaps, too willing to take credit for the ideas or achievements of others? In other words, are you someone people cannot entirely trust?

We all know the popular manager who agrees with everybody publicly but then says and does things his own way once outside the meeting. Or how about the person who backs out of agreed strategies, decisions, or commitments but then signs onto them again when it seems expedient to do so?

There is wisdom in rethinking or reassessing a situation and changing direction when warranted, but there is a fine line between that and sliding in and out of commitments. The former seems strategic, the latter untrustworthy—which was how Lindsay was perceived.

Where do you stand on trust?

CONTROL

The "shadow" or dark side of being organized may be the need to always be in control of everything. What seems to you like being organized, knowing where everything is, and committing to getting things done may seem to others as you being the ultimate control freak.

Take Paul, for example. He thinks he is trying to manage risk so as to exceed performance goals, but to the members of his team, it looks like he is deliberately and inappropriately narrowing their scope of responsibility in an effort to maintain control. Do you control too much or too hard, failing or forgetting to delegate responsibilities or decisions to the appropriate level? If so, you need to reflect on what it is about the situation that makes you act that way. Dig deep into what it is about the other person, the context, or your own needs that makes you hold on to control so tightly.

How can you begin to unclench some control? If you are unsure of the abilities of the people you might normally delegate to, perhaps you need to share your expectations with them more crisply and compellingly. You might work *with* the individual, establishing guidelines, acting as teacher or mentor as you plan together to manage the effort to the levels you need.

If worry about risk has turned you into a control freak, perhaps you can break down the project or effort into smaller, more manageable chunks to limit the risk. At the very least, you can share your concerns with team members so they understand your decision to maintain control.

Maybe the need to be in control is within you. Do you feel as if you're under a microscope? Are you basing current actions on past experiences? Can you test and discard those old memories? Or can you share them with your team so they can help ease your concerns?

Where do you stand on the control issue?

Motivating Passions

You know that getting yourself motivated to deliver on your goals is an art as well as a science. You can set goals with technical precision, but getting yourself to follow through and deliver, not to mention excel, is a complex effort.

So your assessment of the passions that motivate you should focus on both forms: the extrinsic motivation driven by material rewards, and the intrinsic motivation driven by your own sense of accomplishment in a job well done—actually, in a job fantastically done.

In a way, that makes the questions in this self-awareness exercise simple: What turns you on? And what keeps you going when the going gets tough? We all know people who get excited about the impact their product or service will have on the customer, others who are electrified by the nature of the work itself, and still others who dream of turning today's fringe product into tomorrow's blockbuster. Knowing where you fit along this spectrum is essential.

One reason is that the research increasingly shows that you can raise your own intrinsic motivation, literally increase the rewards, based on your enjoyment of what you do—that feeds your inner needs. Knowing how those rewards work for you can keep you focused; you can actually amp up your passion on the job by staying engaged and on track for those rewards.

You should also be aware of the extrinsic factors that motivate you—the things your organization or other sources provide to reward your work. Regular compensation or the financial windfall of a bonus, the sheer high of making the sale, promotions, a corner office, or a new title—whatever it is, and more than likely it is a combination of many factors, be aware of what works for you and of how important each factor is to your individual profile.

Finally, can you visualize success? Being able to do so is vital to sustaining motivation. Remember that your goals are doable, and anticipate what winning will feel like. Here is an exercise that will help.

Passion Mapping

Passion can be an amazing driver of outcomes. It is defined as an intense emotion, a compelling enthusiasm, or desire for something. It's also often infectious—you can get people around you to support your efforts much more easily if you have that twinkle in the eye and the eagerness in the voice that passion often exhibits. You may already know what drives you. For example, Lindsay loved cooking and all things food-related. Knowing her passions helped her hone in on a potential career and work that would intrinsically motivate her. What are your passions?

1. List the Activities or Interests That Excite or Motivate You

Here are some ways to hone in on some of your drivers and passions, though you might find other ways of tracking what drives you.

A. REMEMBER THE CHILD INSIDE YOU

In his poem "The Rainbow," William Wordsworth noted how his childhood shaped his current views and ends with the phrase, "the child is father of the man."[3] In many ways, this is a worthwhile guidance; think back to your favorite activities as a child. I'll confess to being rather a geek. I would spend happy summer afternoons selecting a random volume of the encyclopedia in our library, opening to a random page, and soon I was immersed in the entry on typhoid or Botswana. The written word and new knowledge was the core of my being. As time moved on, writing for its own sake fell by the wayside, but I've had the good fortune of resurrecting that love.

A second element is to watch what you do when you are relaxed and having fun. What do you do when you are not fully scheduled? What do you read about and what TV shows do you watch?

Revisit the activities you enjoyed as a child. Would you enjoy them now? Is there a grown-up version of it?

All of these activities harbor clues to what inspires in you a certain passion. Can they be plotted together, and can they be added into your life now? Are they pointing to a new career option, perhaps?

B. WHO DO YOU WANT TO BE WHEN YOU "GROW UP"?

We talk about role models, but expand beyond them. Are there people you know that you aspire to be? I often look at our friend Shelley Rubin, cofounder and cochair of the Rubin Museum of Art and founder and chair of A Blade of Grass arts foundation, and tell her that I'd love to be her when I grow up. What do I mean? Here is someone who took to technology early, made brave personal choices, contributes generously in her later life to critical social movements, and entertains and connects influencers and mentors them along the way. I know the striving it took but also the deep engagement in social movements that inspires her and me—that's key to all that I do.

Who would you want to be when you grow up? Identify a few, and hone in on what you see in these people that you admire and what passions you share.

Take time to understand how they evolved. Talk to them, Google them, and read their interviews if any exist. Getting in their head to understand the steps to honing in on their success is part of the fun of such an experience.

C. What is your "brain worm"?

You know that tune that refuses to leave you, the "ear worm"? It's irritating, but you wake up in the morning humming it and you find yourself singing the tune in the shower. It's like Peyton Manning's "Nationwide" tune—it's always there.

You'll find that successful people have a small set of questions that keep them going: Would people pay to travel with me to unvisited locations in the world? Would cars drive themselves better than people do? Will happier people really make better employees, and would a company pay for happiness?

Step back and note down all those questions that swirl through your mind; the secret of your passion may be hidden in there.

D. WHAT WERE YOU DOING WHEN YOU WERE IN "FLOW" OR "IN THE ZONE"?

In 1990, psychologist Mihály Csíkszentmihályi wrote about the concept of flow in his book *Flow: The Psychology of Optimal Experience.* He examined artists and other professions where he saw people being most engaged and happiest when they are in a state of flow—a state in which they were so absorbed that nothing else seemed to matter.[4] It's visible in many disciplines; in sports we often call it "being in the zone." I remember those shooting competitions when everything just worked. It's like I didn't have to consciously do anything because the actions and outcomes were almost automatic.

Flow as an idea is reflected in many religions and historic movements. Buddhism and Hinduism talk about a state called doing without doing, which sounds a lot like flow.

Do you remember a time when you felt inspired, when things seemed to come easily and automatically? When were you elated and happiest? Take a note; there is a clue in there.

2. Now, Plot Your Passions on the Map

How might you mix and match them to create a viable working hypothesis for your journey forward? Take a clear-eyed view of all your passions and rate them for their value in a professional context.

Use the R-W-W Innovation Screen developed by Don Schrello, which in essence asks the questions: "Is it real, can we win, and is it worth it?"[5] Companies use them to assess business potential and risk exposure in their innovation portfolios. You can use them to test your passions as well as your ideas.

So ask yourself:

- Real passion: Is there a potential use to my passion? Can I make something of it—a product, service, or consulting capability?
- Winning passion: If I grabbed this passion with both hands, do I have the time and ability to win at whatever I do with it?
- Worthwhile passion: How will this passion pay for itself? Will it be worth it?

That's exactly what Lindsay tested as she went into discussions about her app.

Why do motivating passions matter? In the next few chapters, we'll start planning how you can build on yours to make them viable future career opportunities.

The Discomfort of Digging Deep

Is digging deep easy? No. Although a realistic view of where you are right now is the essential first step to jolting your career forward and upward, it can be, as Lindsay found, a difficult and possibly even dispiriting process.

For one thing, professionals tend to slip into a set of assumptions about themselves and the value they bring to the table. Dismissing those assumptions and taking an unvarnished look inside can be uncomfortable; it may dredge up issues you don't quite feel ready to address. But just as an organization needs an honest analysis of what it is and has before it embarks on a program of change, growth, or expansion, you need to take on the tough issues now. Doing so will give you both a head start on jolting your life and the confidence to make the jolt work. You wouldn't be reading this book if you didn't want the jolt to work well.

Honesty, even if hurtful, is precisely what you are after in this self-assessment. Identifying and understanding just how you inhabit each of the three spheres—core capabilities, black holes, and motivating passions—is precisely how you can define who you are. And who you are is your starting point for jolting your career forward and upward. To address where you stand in each of the three spheres with anything less than total honesty does a disservice to you and your career. It simply won't get the job of jolting your career done.

It isn't easy to ask colleagues, friends, peers, and team members to answer some tough questions you put to them. They may initially be taken aback by the questions, so keep in mind that they will also appreciate your seeking their honest opinion. That is why it's important to ask specific questions, not just a general "So, how am I doing?" Such questions are easier for your interviewees to respond to, and they are the only kinds of questions that produce the results you seek.

Listen carefully to what your interviewees say; make sure you're not just waiting for your turn to speak. You can ask all the questions in the world, but if you don't hear what people tell you, you can't benefit from their input.

Confirm what you think you heard. People appreciate being given the opportunity to clarify what they've said, especially if it's off the cuff. It's also better for your own jolt planning to understand exactly what they see as your strengths, motivations, and black holes. That way, you're not making plans based on wrong information. As you have evolved and grown as a professional, you may have slipped into thinking you know what your value is in the organization and marketplace—that's a complacency that could come to haunt you. Always check.

It is never easy to sit down and reflect inwardly. It's up to you to think about what you know about yourself and what you've heard from others—their perceptions of you. Remember those moments that have surprised you: the meeting when your ideas didn't go too far or the team member who didn't seem to "get with the program." Does the information you now have begin to explain some of what happened?

The good news associated with this potentially painful self-assessment exercise is simply that people *can* change. In fact, we humans do it all the time. Personality or character "types" catalogued through the decades can be a useful shorthand for communicating across teams and with individuals. But your own "type" is really only a takeoff point from which to start working on your growth and development.

Meanwhile, the emerging field of neuroplasticity has shown that, like any muscle, even the adult brain—the power behind all your actions—can evolve and grow through both exercise and practice. One simple but striking example comes from a study of London's legendary cab drivers. The study shows that their hippocampi—the part of the brain that handles spatial memory tasks—were measurably larger than those of bus drivers.[6] The reason? London taxi drivers are required to memorize a map of the city with its 25,000 streets and thousands of landmarks. While bus drivers generally drive the same route every day, the cabbies constantly rely on this part of the brain to navigate the maze of London streets and get their passengers where they want to go. It is confirmation for any adult that it really is possible to acquire new skills and gain new capabilities simply by trying.

That should make it a bit easier to dig deep.

Put Your Self-Awareness Map to Work *Now*

Don't *just* assess. As you discover things about yourself you'd like to change, begin the transformation. Let self-awareness inspire you, and let inspiration incite action. Establish goals and metrics for yourself based on what you hear in the interviews and the meaning you take from that, and make sure you can monitor the metrics yourself, without having to go back to the people you've interviewed. For example, you may decide to work on your control needs. How about simply setting a goal of halving the number of follow-ups you take on versus delegate? That is, for each project, force yourself to start identifying others who will take on more of the action items. Yes, it's going to be difficult initially, but you will be developing your team's capability. You may decide to take a step at a time and build some "insurance" or guard rails, but hand things off as much as you can.

Then, track your progress toward the goals on a monthly, quarterly, and annual basis to ensure they stay top-of-mind for you. This self-monitoring will help you develop behaviors that become part of your normal way of working and being in the world.

Finally, stay flexible. Don't be afraid to evolve your thinking and to change your actions. That's what the jolt is all about.

CHAPTER 3

Discipline #2: Stalk Innovations and Trends

If now is the time, then what is the space? Where do you start even thinking about creating the career you want? After all, these days industries seem to have the life span of a fruit fly. Remember creating playlists on CDs and renting movies in a video store? Remember personal secretaries and graphics departments? Very soon now, we're likely to be asking if you remember broadcast television—not long after that, cable television. And what happens to the career paths in each of these industries?

Our profound economic transition also means a wildly dynamic business environment. It's hard to plot a career change if you're not sure the industry you're planning on will be there when you jolt. Keeping up with context is a serious and difficult challenge.

Now Trending . . .

The task is to distinguish between fashions and trends and, if possible, to catch them early. Let's put it this way: Fashions rage, and then fade. Trends start as waves, and then become currents. Fashions are not worth wasting time on; trends are what you want to focus on as you look for the place where you can jolt your career forward and upward. To find them, watch for changes that start showing up in multiple arenas of life. Remember when you dismissed Twitter as a way to share what you ate? Remember the day you watched all the social interactions, and realized that this can be a force of change and an opportunity? It may have taken the Arab Spring to see the power of social platforms, but some people and companies have learned to harness social media to drive great results for themselves. So keep your eyes open, and make sure you're not building walls but are paying attention to the trends.

Checkpoint: Survey Insights

Our survey of 300 innovators showed that most people found working with teams critical for ideation and innovation execution, but 40 percent took on two specific tasks at a more individual level: identifying trends and seeing and translating weak signals.

Although there is a place for teamwork here, individuals seem to take more responsibility for the early part of inspiration—seeing something emerge and understanding its implications.

This chapter lays out some of the trends today, but it is just a start to help making you more sensitive to emerging trends.

No book can point you to the specific trends that will shape the context of your individual career. What I can and will do in this book is point out those currents that I believe suggest new—sometimes *radically* new—directions.

I've packaged these suggestions into a list at the end of this chapter. As it happens, Lindsay's jolt addressed a couple of these currents.

A Five-Step Plan

How did she do it? Lindsay took five steps to create her jolt and bottle her luck—five actions that prepared her for her leap into a different career trajectory by getting her to reframe the way she looked at her work life and its context. *She* did the reframing, including the digging, the exploring, the gathering of data and resources, the testing and challenging, the imagining, the retesting, and re-challenging. So will you. Here's how:

1. As you saw in the last chapter, you start by digging deep to examine your own skills, capabilities, and resources so you can honestly assess the value you bring to the market, as well as your own attitudes toward what constitutes success and how to measure growth.

2. You then explore the context in which you can offer this value, and you do this by tracking market innovations and

emerging trends and deciphering what they might mean to you. *You'll find a good start to this in the 10 career currents listed at the end of this chapter.*

3. In the next few chapters you will take on the other steps. You activate all your assets—including your networks of associates and acquaintances who can drive significant value for you—to add other perspectives to what you've learned from looking inward and from stalking the market.

4. Prototype the possibilities for yourself and then test-drive them. Challenge everything you've come up with; run it through a meat grinder of fact- and reality-checking to make sure you haven't left anything out and that what you have come up with is real.

5. Go extreme; run that final reality check and jump. Can this future be achieved, by you, at this time? Once you've answered yes, you're ready. And once you're ready, leap! Jolt your career out of today and into the future.

Lindsay knew that her market value was her competence; whatever the project was, she could get it done. But she wasn't interested in the same career in a different organization; she had a fresh vision for her life, one guided by her passions. She wanted to find a context and a role within that context that would be dominated and shaped by those passions: food and travel.

Lindsay began exploring trends and innovations in the farm-to-table movement, the expanding role of executive chefs and owner-chefs, culinary tourism, travel writing, travel apps, and sites like TripAdvisor that drive tourists to new kinds of experiences. She talked to anyone from the worlds of food and travel who would listen, and she listened to anyone who would talk. It was a time-consuming process, and Lindsay spent the time, seeing it as an investment in her future.

Eventually, she thought she saw a possibility, namely, homing in on the ultra-wealthy, a group with whom her job made her familiar. How might she provide this select group, with its considerable resources for sophisticated experiences in travel and cuisine, something appealingly new? Was it custom-tailored restaurant evenings or custom-tailored travel experiences? Was it custom-tailored dining while on a custom-tailored trip?

Wait a minute. Who was she kidding? Were her online skills really up to it? Could she shift her command of vast technology resources at a huge corporation to a home-computing setup and an individual business purpose, one that would pass the taste test of the ultra-wealthy? Did she have the energy to establish an innovative business? Was her Rolodex of contacts sufficient to build an offering, and was she comfortable activating the Rolodex? Lindsay challenged her own idea—up, down, and sideways.

And she adjusted it. She began with a blowout notion of specialized consulting to the ultra-wealthy—a one-woman shop providing entrée into a vast array of possibilities and ideas she would have at her fingertips. She wrung that idea through the fact- and reality-checking challenge and trimmed and refined it down to three possibilities: one, an easy jolt that let her slide into the travel-and-cuisine industry by working for a player within it—either on the media end of the industry or in the travel arrangement sector; two, creating an app specifically for the target she had in mind, in hopes of selling it to a company like TripAdvisor; and three, designing her own Website featuring executive chefs who would curate tours to exotic locations.

She tasted a morsel of each possibility by undertaking a specific action in each. She tested the waters of employment at travel publishing groups and travel arrangement agencies and found both industries to be in what looked to her like a moment of retrenching and confusion. She sketched out an app that offered the kind of service she would like. And she contacted executive chefs about a possible Website. All these possibilities had their pros and cons, pluses and minuses.

Once she had a taste of each, it was time for a final reality check. For which jolt did Lindsay have the fire in her belly, the financial wherewithal, and whatever else it might take at this time?

Lindsay found partners to help fund the app she had sketched; it enabled users to tap into specialized cultural and culinary experiences—in just one exotic region of the world to start with. Meanwhile, she stayed in her job at the bank; it seemed a good hinge-point from which to keep tabs on the app and her market.

It was a little jolt, Lindsay will tell you, and only the first. Still, this small, exciting shift in her career trajectory seemed to her full of potential and a good platform for a later jolt that could take her to who knows where. In this case, size didn't matter; "small" was sufficient to make Lindsay feel liberated and on her way to a new place in her life.

We'll catch up with her later. For now, it's time to focus on how to create your own jolt, one step at a time.

Take Action: Be a Trend-Seeking Panther

Trend-seeking is about watching, waiting, and stalking trends purposefully. A trend signifies a general direction in which something is developing or changing. Being hyper-aware of trends makes sure you are less likely to be taken by surprise when the change itself happens or becomes the norm.

Once you have realized what you're passionate about and what your goals are, stalk the trends in and around your space and gather information. It's impossible to know everything out there, but look at trends around you that pertain to your career. Whether you are talking to people, reading the newspapers, or walking down the street, it's about recognizing trends. For example, if you can't go to industry conferences, look up the agenda and look at the topics of discussion for trend ideas in your space.

Trends are often the combination of four drivers:

- Technologies that are evolving and being developed or discovered at all times, whether they are high-science technologies like nanotechnology or software-based technologies like the software platforms that power new robotics and artificial intelligence agents.

- Needs or wants that propel innovators to use technologies to address a human need or a consumer want; for example, clean water or cheaper rides to work.
- Norms and practices that evolve as the technologies and needs come together, such as a greater interest in sharing resources, hence the sharing economy; or greater acceptance of unconventional materials, such as when desalination plants are funded because people no longer reject sea water as a source for drinking water.
- Jolts that amp up the importance of the three factors—technology, needs/wants, and norms/practices—so that what seems like a marginal fashion becomes a real trend.

1. Watch the Details: The 360 View

A panther on the hunt is constantly watching and uses its broader visual field to take in as much of the details as possible.

Trends might appear on the streets, malls, and cafes around you way before they reach the business world or mainstream. Successful innovators decode these emerging insights into something solid—a product or fashion—that is accessible to the rest of us.

In soccer, you'll hear the coach telling the kids to keep their heads on a swivel. It's not about just watching the ball, but looking to see what else is happening on the field, with the opponent as well as team members, constantly watching for emerging opportunities for how to win or place the ball for maximum effect.

Similarly, wherever you are—in meetings, at a conference, the park, or at the movies, for example—you should ask yourself, what's happening here? Do you see new ads? Are people spending their time or money differently? Is the language around you shifting? What are "the kids" doing?

Use your travels well; what's different and why? I remember seeing chips embedded in credit cards in Europe more than six years before they arrived in the United States. The way bills were being paid and the level of security in seeing the billing happening right at your table changed interactions and speed of service significantly. Those point-of-sale machines soon came stateside at the Apple store, for example.

2. Read Deep, Broad, and Around the Edges

Take your time to immerse yourself in a topic, but select a couple of books and read them in-depth. Early in my time thinking about this book, I remember filling my travel time reading *Iconoclast* by Gregory Berns and *Hacker, Hoaxer, Whistleblower, Spy: The Many Faces of Anonymous* by Gabriella Coleman, each telling of fascinating mental models and actions driven by mental orientation.

In addition, prioritize a broad read every day. If you still get the newspapers, for example, take the time to skim from front to back. Connect the dots on how economic forces, social movements, technology, and political actions fit together and drive each other. We're still working through the impact of social media, social unrest, and political aspirations that drove the Arab Spring and opened the way for increasing political fragmentation.

Read around the edges as well. Use social media tools and consider using trend-tracking tools like

Google Trends, which captures search and news trends, or BuzzFeed, which is an irreverent trend tracker that highlights the Web's most viral memes.

3. Ask Your Fellow Panthers

Engage with others as well. Creating the right networks is part of the story—check with your LinkedIn communities and Twitter followers. Also, find reputable experts you can trust to be smart, reliable, and have valuable opinions. Explore blogs that examine the trends you're seeing; usually there's someone obsessing about anything you're interested in. Be selective and filter out the noise, of course. Most importantly, don't forget your competitors or peers. They are likely to be watching trends in interesting nooks and crannies that will affect your space and industry.

4. Participate in the Action: Hang Out With Purpose

Reach out to the trendsetters and watch what they do. They are daring and experimental, thinking outside the box, and competing with each other for the most groundbreaking insights. Just as academic disciplines are melding, so are the influencers. Media moguls, fashion icons, and scientists hang out and engage; they are social animals with a great sense of style and cutting edge.

If you can, prioritize one or more conferences a year. Don't just go to the usual keynotes—find the panels where the innovators are talking. Go where you are uncomfortable and you'll learn a lot more than going to the usual industry hangouts.

5. Scribe Your Insights

Keep notes. Strive to identify the problems that lots of people will be happy to pay to solve *or* opportunities that open up new markets, behaviors, or systems. Keep a look-out to filter out fads slowly, and start developing storylines that play out how the trends will "pop," that is, come together to make a real change happen. If you're in a company or trying to develop customers, share your storylines with your teams or competitors to see if they will help fund experiments or the development of solutions. Otherwise, you can plan to go it alone.

Remember, don't expect your insights to pop up in a moment. This is about tracking the 25 things happening through time that will lead to your lightbulb moment. Once you start seeing trends that could affect your career, ask questions such as: Why is this relevant? How could this be relevant? What am I going to do with this insight?

Go With the Flow?
Ten Career Currents with Potent Potential to Consider *Today!*

Retail is a pervasive force in all our lives, and whether it's the context of your current career or not, its sheer pervasiveness makes it something of a bellwether for the wider marketplace. That makes this sector worth exploring, both on its own and as a significant predictor of what may be coming soon to a marketplace more specific to your own work.

Trending now in retail is the ever-increasing porousness of the customer experience. Both the brick-and-mortar store and the online shopping experience are up for grabs. In what seems an increasingly distracted world, retail has come to mean being inspired around the dinner table, making a quick search on a mobile phone, deeper research later that evening on the Website, and then possibly a visit to the store during the weekend to test it out. But that doesn't mean the store is the point of purchase. Back home again and back online, there's the urge to research price comparisons, and while there, maybe just place the order before bedtime. Or maybe not. Just forget about it.

The research tells us that about 68 percent of online carts are abandoned, and 25 percent of customers surveyed say that's because the navigation was too complicated.[1] Creating a sticky, productive online experience is not a simple task, so what is emerging as an adjunct to the porous customer experience is a shift in the way retailers market themselves.

Specifically, the trend is to do more storytelling than selling. This is not an original idea. Revlon founder Charles Revson said it a century ago: "In the factory, we make cosmetics; in the store, we sell hope."[2] It works. I remember my first weekend in New York City at the turn of this century, when I stopped dead in front of a Saks Fifth Avenue display window and was enveloped by a woodland fantasy that instantly wove a story in my mind. Yes, what was being sold was the evening gown, the shoes, and the clutch, but they were just accessories to the statement about luxury, confidence, and power emanating from the story in the window.

With the kind of access retailers have today to customer behavior data—through cookies, loyalty programs, and mobile connections—they can harness the information for effective market segmentation and develop segment-specific and nuanced elements of the storyline. In time, they may be able to individualize each storyline. What is essential is that the core of the story be anchored to the value the retailer can provide to the customer.

Uniqlo is my favorite example of a retailer that embodies these possibilities, consistently achieving its own differentiated storyline. Enter its New York flagship store, and embedded screens everywhere you look remind you that this is all about fashionable, affordable clothes and outerwear made of highly innovative fabrics. The Website-like experience is underscored by the subtle use of color and space; each step takes you into a new color zone or related line of clothing. Customer service is always a click or step away; the staff all carry handhelds and can tell you where your dream Uniqlo coat is—downstairs or on the Web.

There are other examples: the Genius Bar at Apple, where focused problem-solvers underscore the storyline of technology first and customer close behind; the transformation of tired, remote Burberry into a compelling luxury leader, using social media to round out a whiz-bang online experience focused on more than 10 million Facebook followers. But in general, plugging the holes in the porous customer experience by finding the story and telling it well remains a work in progress for the vast retail market, and makes the industry a place to watch for changes to the context of your career.

Education, which I understand to mean the development of capabilities at any age, continues to experience fits and starts as it seeks the right working model for a range of learning circumstances. A prime example is MOOCs—massive open online courses—which flared with great fanfare as a way to redefine access to information and expertise, then quietly fizzled.

But the solutions are out there, and the purpose is fabulous. Imagine a smart young child in a village in India learning from a professor at a university in California, then connecting with a similarly talented student in Germany for research. Or consider the potential for businesses that can leverage learning technologies to continually develop workers' talents and remain poised at all times for market changes and innovation. It all makes education a space to be watched.

Visualization and communication—integrated as one—constitute another field that is about to break wide open in unprecedented ways. An analysis of a decade of Web searches across the United States revealed, among other fascinating conclusions, that in the easiest places in the country in which to live—the wealthiest and most advanced—cameras are what people most often search for information on.[3] Now come miniaturization and integration with all sorts of tools, giving us helmet cameras, cop videos, drones, and many more devices and providing virtually immediate recording and transmitting of a range of interactions. It makes this sphere an area to focus on through the lens of your own work and career.

Home management is another sphere ripe for takeoff well beyond the current use of smartphones and tablets to turn on or off music, lighting, thermostats, and locks. Watch for emerging trends in home-based energy and security.

Just as fertile a field for emerging trends is the "reference-ability" embodied by Angie's List, a review service of home-improvement companies designed to take the angst out of hiring contractors. As of this writing, Angie's List serves up reviews in 500 categories, primarily of home and healthcare services. But the increasing use of networks and systems to provide references is becoming more prevalent even in smaller commercial jobs. It is a trend to watch.

Cloud computing is a core trend that is making a meaningful difference in the way small- and medium-sized businesses can operate and is, thus, also making a difference in the number of these smaller businesses. When a one-member organization can remotely access the same kinds of financial systems, customer relations management systems, and communication systems used by the corporate behemoths, then all sorts of new possibilities open up. So keep an eye out on trends in cloud computing.

And keep an eye on the *nomad economy* which is the trend toward increasing numbers of Americans working for themselves, a trend that says as much about the future of full-time work in large enterprises as it does about lifestyle choices among freelancers. In 2013, the Federal Reserve Bank of New York named Freelancers Union founder and executive director Sara Horowitz to its board of directors—a clear recognition of the important role played by the "independent workers" who constitute one-third of America's workforce. They may constitute a market unto themselves.

Is there an *entrepreneurship ecosystem*? Talent tends to go where there are other professionals and a customer base. But those places are only the beginning. UNESCO's Netexplo observatory is a network of more than 200 journalists, scientists, and academics who detect outstanding initiatives in Internet and digital technology everywhere on the planet. Since 2008, the group has recognized the creators of the 100 most significant changes already at work in society. Among them are Kenya-based Ushahidi, which builds open-source software tools and runs a platform for access to the Web; the justice crowdsourcing site and app SocialCops from India; and the digital taste generator, called the digital lollipop from Singapore. Entrepreneurship ecosystems make these initiatives possible.

By all means, keep an eye on the ***sharing economy*** and the world of experiences it represents. Although sharing has been part of commerce for ages (remember the lending library?), Internet technology has now made the sharing of services and physical assets a breeze. One obvious example is the plethora of online U.S. sites like RelayRides and GetAround—peer-to-peer car rental mechanisms that allow you to hire your neighbors' cars for however long you need wheels. Unused cars are now a service members get paid for. What's interesting about this is that RelayRides doesn't own any inventory, has a self-renewing supply, can easily expand geographically by adding a few servers, and allows the community of users to serve as quality control through the reputation management part of the Website. That's a good working model for addressing the reality that people may be more interested in the use of a product than in the product itself. It means that selling the product use as a service is an emerging priority, whereas renting from other consumers is as viable as renting from a company. It's definitely a trend to watch.

The ***intersection of mobile access and big data*** is another sphere in which emerging trends may change the context of your work life. The emerging markets of the third and fourth worlds have, perforce, been the pioneers in this, with key services like news and banking being the front-runners in innovating mobile services for expanding access to mobile devices. But as smartphones grow ever cheaper, the meeting point of access, apps, and data represents a range of new possibilities. Studies of U.S. technology usage, for example, have tracked a steady decline in time spent on the computer versus a corresponding increase in time spent accessing the Internet on mobile phones.[4] For businesses that can monitor their customers' behaviors and preferences, the intersection of mobile access and big data means not just smarter operating decisions, but innovation as well. It is how Uber can modify its pricing on the spot, surge-pricing to allocate cars to the highest paying customer as demand increases. It's a new business model and a space to keep an eye on.

Finally, watch for trends in the *health* sphere, a sphere that, at the time of this writing, is transforming at a rapid rate. We've all seen the various forms of "body candy"—wearable technology—combined with telemedicine to offer real-time monitoring of your health. We've seen various attempts at using handhelds for access to your health records. But keep an eye also on such emerging trends as bone-induction hearing aids (that is, vibrating your skull to communicate the sound into your inner ear), and on health start-ups like MiSeq that seek to make genome sequencing accessible to small organizations and individuals. The sci-fi vision of surgery performed remotely across the ocean is stunning, but closer to reality are the possibilities for extending care from major medical centers to far-flung rural areas underserved by healthcare providers because they are simply too hard to reach. This is real transformation.

Take Action: Stalk Trends!

Periodically, work through this exercise to push your thinking and make sure your observations of trends begin to feel more concrete.

Use some of the scenario planning and option analysis exercises that a company would use, but from a more personal perspective.

1. Keep a virtual trend book; clip articles or maintain a diary of interesting trends. What's happening that intrigues you?

> What are the data points you should keep in mind? When does a seeming anomaly become a trend? For example, when did farm-to-table become "a thing"? Was it when your mom started shopping at farmers' markets or when chains like Chipotle start sourcing as much at 85 percent of their product at local farms?
>
> 2. Design "new worlds." Consider two trends that seem pertinent to you or match your passions and areas of interest.
>
> 3. Evaluate the trends. Do you believe they are here to stay? How would you measure these trends, or set the trend scale, that is, assess how to measure the observable impact of the trend? For example, if farm-to-table truly takes off, what kind of revenue will that open up for local farms?

In Lindsay's case, she knew foodies were spending more on experiences, and high-net worth travel experiences were becoming a reality. Understanding how much that spending was growing and exploring how the travel world would evolve was part of her exercise.

Now describe this scenario and how you see it playing out for you. In Lindsay's case, you may consider the following story to be a possibility. As Americans learn more about cuisines and cooking from TV shows and travel, they have begun to visit restaurants especially for the celebrity chef and exotic cuisines. In addition, curated experiences have been on the rise, whether they are special safaris designed for the avid photographer or the innovation tours around hot business centers. A few travel agencies have begun to craft wine tours and specialty cheese tours.

The potential to design and market high-end food tours is pretty tempting!

Describe the scenario or the new world. For example, Lindsay tested the idea that even high-net worth clients would use apps for research, but also that curated travel experiences would be a sustainable business.

Identify specific actions you can take for succeeding in this "new world":

- How could I fit into this trend or scenario?
- How could I benefit in this market (money, social impact, etc.)?
- What kinds of people would I need to surround myself with to succeed

(mentors, guides, partners, future employees, etc.)?

- What other capabilities would I need to develop to better capitalize on these trends or this new world?
- How could I finance this new world?
- What activities would I need to stop doing to be successful?

CHAPTER 4

Discipline #3: Your Network on Jolt!

When I first met James (a composite), I was impressed by his business card and puzzled by the haunted look in his eyes. The two simply didn't go together. The card said he was a top leader in a powerhouse organization, but the handshake and diffident "hello" said this was a troubled guy. Ten minutes into our chat, I understood why. The haunted look came from the pressures James faced—and from the fact that he knew he was not firing on all cylinders as he confronted those pressures. Halfway through a career that up to this point had been stellar and fulfilling, James felt he had reached the end of the line.

James had been at an international retail giant for 20 years. He had come up through the ranks and was well loved by the manufacturing and operations personnel he had always worked with. His expertise was unequaled, and he was known for having eased his division through a number of crises with great success. When a new CEO took over, it was not surprising that James caught the leadership's eye. He was tapped to be the global leader for the firm's largest and fastest-growing division, serving its premier clients. Simply put, he was tasked to lead a huge business into a still unknown future—a job well away from his comfort zone as the shepherd of processes and systems.

But it was the plum assignment—the one that everyone wanted—and James knew it. He also knew that the assignment was a vote of confidence. He would now be interacting with the mover-and-shaker clients. At first, he assumed that the well-oiled machine of the organization would need only a light hand, but it didn't take long for him to realize that his skills weren't enough to move his new division as far and as fast as it needed to move. Six months into his new role, he was starting to feel the heat. His boss had hoped to see him rid the division of its non-productive staff, speed up the use of new technologies that had been purchased from start-ups, and attract new clients. Instead, James couldn't stop looking through the rearview mirror as he fought fires ignited by ineffective talent and wrong business moves. He spent much of his time taking customer complaint calls while trying to convince the leadership he was the right leader in the role. It went a long way toward explaining his hunted look. And it is what prompted James to seek out my assistance.

We began by identifying what was working and what was not working, and delving into why. As we unraveled the situation, James could see that he lacked an innovative vision for his division. His outlook had become insular. Effective and contented within his group of engineering buddies, he had not bothered to attend many of the corporate events that might have empowered him to step up his game, and he tended to avoid rooms where he didn't know everything. He chose his own leadership team from among his limited set of loyal followers, many of whom had never worked in any other organization and therefore, like James, knew little about other ways of working. Most important, James continued to think and talk like an operational engineer—eyes on the mechanism at hand and not looking to the future. And that is how he was seen.

He saw that he needed to make some new investments in his own development so that he could originate the kind of innovative vision required of his position. Networking was the way James would "fund" those investments.

James worked with his assistant to map out six conferences for the year. The conference fees added up, which motivated James to rolodex methodically all the great new people he was meeting and the insights he was capturing in those meetings. In the past, James had been laser-focused on selling business; now, however, he was actively seeking three categories of people: "upstarts" who were trying to upset the apple cart in how they thought about the industry, people who "did not look like him" in their expertise and pedigree, and thought leaders he would meet with periodically to see where the new thinking was. In the process, James had learned to get beyond his focus on operational priorities as, almost without knowing it, he became a listener and a delegator—life was about the possibilities, not the next operational target.

It's hard to overestimate the importance of network impact in the business climate in which we all work today. Ours is now a world of relationships rather than transactions, and those relationships can be particularly decisive when you are weighing options, charting bold moves, or trying to build out a new service line. As you work with others in various ways, through changing roles and in shifting dynamics—sometimes as equals, sometimes in a client relationship, and sometimes as collaborators—you develop a genuine reciprocity; you know you're going to "meet" again in another role and a different dynamic, so you need to take the long view of a relationship. It's not about the latest billable minute; it's about the next brainstorm that can benefit either or both of you equally.

You've been diligent in laying out your strengths, interests, passions, and blind spots. You've acknowledged that there are some things that come easier than others, and that there are blind spots you might wish to work on.

You've considered innovative trends that may have an impact on your area(s) of interest.

In this chapter, we'll work on helping you build the kind of network that strong, successful innovators develop with time. The best networks accentuate strengths, mitigate blind spots, and amplify passion; they are the wind beneath the wings of innovators. Networking comes naturally to some, but it's a skill that can be learned and developed through time.

Here's what we'll discuss in the next few pages:

1. Determine the state of your network.
2. Mine your current network for impact.
3. Create network opportunities and amp up your network.
4. Actively build your network strategically to help you create the jolt you seek.
5. Finally, provocatively engage your network as the honest outsider. Take advantage of your current role being a little outside the role you are hoping to play. Use your objectivity to design a new way of thinking about the possibilities.

Checkpoint: Survey Insights

Entrepreneurs often (35 percent) identified networking as a primary strength, as did people who identified their primary role as developing ideas (40 percent). This stands in comparison with only 18 percent of the overall population, who also don't seem to view networking as part of their job.

Idea generators are also very active in using their network across the social/professional setting and for new idea testing—65 percent of them do, versus 45 percent of the larger group.

Additionally, a majority of respondents (67 percent) find they generate new ideas in groups and with their networks. The vast majority of new idea generators (64 percent) had networks of more than 50 individuals that they ideate with.

As the world of work evolves, information is more broadly accessible. However, asymmetries also continue to widen, and networks seem to be the difference between how entrepreneurs and ideators succeed, versus the broader population.

Your career connections will always be an important piece to moving ahead. Consider your goals and think about who you know. Do you know someone who has expertise in your area of interest? If not, are there others who might connect you with someone who does? When was the last time you connected?

I. Assess the State of Your Network

Okay, dear reader, get out your highlighter and do a simple "Cosmo"-like survey with me. To those of you who have been safe from the impact of pop culture, I mean the short surveys featured in magazines like *Cosmopolitan* (or "Cosmo") that ask a few questions to drive to insights. Whereas those quizzes aim to help you with such "interesting insights" as whether your spouse is faithful, the surveys here try to do a lot more! Ask yourself what kind of a networker you are—strong, medium, or weak? Take a look at Table 4.1 on pages 116 and 117. Dig deep here, and highlight the descriptions that best reflect you and your networking approach.

II. Mine Your Current Network for Impact

Now you will work on sharpening your networking antennae and provide yourself a benchmark for future networking. This step is all about mapping your current network; I remember creating a visual map from my LinkedIn contacts, using one of their Beta apps that is no longer accessible. Maybe they'll resuscitate it someday or you could use add-on services like Socilab to pull your LinkedIn data. But you can just take a piece of paper and map the folks you are most in touch with. Figure out what their area of specialty is and how they might be able to support your own growth.

When I used one of LinkedIn's add-on tools to map my LinkedIn contacts, the image that emerged looked like a multi-colored flower. The contacts clumped up mostly into four petal-like clusters. One was a pink clump that tended to be organizational specialists and consultants; then came an orange group of pharma executives; a third clump of bankers were highlighted in blue, and then came my journalist friends in deep orange. In essence, if I were to decide to become an angel investor in health start-ups, there would be about 25 experts I could tap to generate the kind of advice I'd need to test my idea. Get my drift? What does your network tell you?

If you are going to map your network, here's a way to capture it. Use your insights from your work with Table 4.1. Be thoughtful about the people you know. This is not a judgmental exercise. Everyone

Table 4.1
Your Networking Approach

STRONG	MEDIUM	WEAK
	Inside work	
• You have friendly relationships with many people at work—i.e., you enjoy discussing both work-related issues as well as common interests unrelated to your work activities. • You know something about each other's lives outside of work. • You are supportive of each other; colleagues depend on you for results and regard you as consistently helpful, dependable, and competent or vice versa. • You know a lot of people you can call on for work-related information or assistance in getting a problem solved. • Your network extends into most areas of the organization.	• You have a few people at work with whom you discuss common interests and share information about life outside of work. • Most interactions on the job relate to the business at hand. • Though you are friendly with people you work with closely, relationships with others are not as positive. Some colleagues may view you as uncooperative or undependable. • There are some people outside your immediate work group that you could call on for information or assistance in getting a problem solved. However, there are a number of areas where it's a bit of a black box.	• Almost all of conversation at work is about business. • You hardly ever talk about your personal life or nonwork activities. You may like your colleagues, but you know little about them. • When you have to work closely with others, the relationship often becomes difficult. There are frequent arguments and disagreements. • There are very few people outside your immediate work group who you know and can reach out to. You are not clear how you could even figure out whom to call in some of these areas.

Outside work		
• You make sure to have at least one event or nonwork-related outside engagement—lunch, coffee, breakfast—with someone who can expose you to a new area or new thinking. • You prioritize and plan network-building activities all the time. You routinely say hello, share relevant articles or interesting information, and wish people well on personal anniversaries or holidays. • You spend some time online daily, whether re-tweeting someone you are following, or posting something on LinkedIn. You stay on top of what's happening on your online networks. • You know who the players are in the space you want to play in. This understanding will help augment and align your networking efforts. • You find ways to give back to the industry in which you work for at least an hour a week. This can take many different forms, from speaking at conferences to writing for journals to simply attending industry events or more.	• You try to schedule networking events, but when push comes to shove, you find a reason to stay at work or go home. Networking often takes the back seat. • You keep track of people, but only reach out when you are facing career transitions or need advice. • You have online profiles, but you are hardly ever active on them. You are more of a watcher than an active participant. • You have a general sense of the companies and a few thinkers in your space, but haven't spent time understanding some of the younger/newer movers and shakers. • You have memberships in key industry groups, but don't often have or take the time to get out to events or be present in forums.	• You are the one willing to make up for the lack of resources on your team. You believe that being internally focused will pay off. No need for external networking. • You know what some of the key networking methods are, but will get to them only if you ever need a new job. • Online networks are a waste of time. • You'll figure out who is important in your industry if you need to for a concrete, work-related reason. • You know there are some industry organizations out there, but you haven't prioritized knowing what events are out there. And often, you ask what the groups can do for you, rather than considering what you can do for the group.

in your network is precious, but some will be part of your *jolt* adventure, and others will applaud you on. Know where you will focus your jolt!

Table 4.4
James' Contact Priorities

Capability/Industry	Your actions	Area: James' example— Visionary leadership
Expert who could provide insights	Engage and learn	*The CEO of James' company was famous for putting out "moon shot" challenges and then giving very light guidance— so she made the list.*
Connector who could provide context and contacts	Understand their focus, build genuine trust	*James met the head of a museum board, and was instantly connected into a network of senior execs who were open to mentoring him.*
Not clear what their value might be	Understand their value, engage	*James knew his peer in the consumer division was supposed to have this profile, but chose to watch him rather than doing anything more active.*
Low network value	Social contact	*James prioritized his alumni network, because even if they are not directly relevant today, he knew that the social impact of staying in touch might have longer-term value for them and him.*

III. Create Networking Priorities and Amp Up Your Network Impact

How is Your Networking Approach chart (Table 4.1) looking? If your table is mostly marked up on the left-hand (STRONG) column, you're doing great! If, on the other hand, like most people, you're all over the place, start a short list of priorities based on the areas where you could do better by focusing on what's in the left-hand column.

Networking puts you in touch with a striking diversity of individuals but builds on shared values. It is shared values that make it possible to get things done together fast or in a tricky situation when a tough call needs to be made.

With Whom Should You Network?

In my view, there are two basic criteria for that. The first is expertise—that is, the people who have a special or unique understanding of pockets of your industry or market. Typically, these individuals tend to be consultative rather than prescriptive and take an iterative approach to problem-solving. Chances are they are curious and suspect there's a better solution ahead; you'll want to make use of that curiosity to get them to collaborate with you. The problem is that such expertise is not always obvious, so the trick is to keep your eyes and ears open both around your organization and in your social circles so you can spot the people who have the expertise, identify them, and then reach out to them.

The second criterion is what I call the airport test. That is, it's nine at night, you're in an airport a million miles from home trying to get to a key meeting the next day, it is snowing like crazy and flights are being cancelled left and right, and your sole companion is the staffer from corporate communications who your boss thought ought to go along to the meeting. If your plane is grounded and you and this individual have to share a taxi to the airport hotel, dine together in the airport hotel restaurant, and maybe have a nightcap together in the airport hotel bar, will you go crazy from irritation, boredom, or both—or will you be okay? In other words, a network comprising people you enjoy being around and who enjoy being around you is probably going to be a strong and effective network.

Here's a simple exercise to start prioritizing areas and identifying people who can help you build out a network or who you can cultivate to connect with. This is just a directional tool—don't "stalk" these contacts! Reach out, be genuine, share your aspirations, and maybe they'll be excited to be part of your network.

Table 4.5
James' Overall Network Map

Dig Deep Profile	Expertise: What is the unique area you'd like to build out based on your Dig Deep Profile?	People / groups to connect with
Key Capabilities (Strengths that can drive affinity—what can you offer?)	*Example: James understood how to engineer solutions.*	*James could connect with MIT Media Lab leads.*
Capability Gaps (What you need to learn.)	*Example: James wasn't a visionary— he struggled with the "big idea."*	*Could attending TED meetings put him in touch with big thinkers?*
Passions (What excited you?)	*Example: James loves robotics.*	*Reaches out to the leading robotics professor at Harvard to explore emerging ideas.*
Blind spots (What do you need to mitigate?)	*James was surprised when he first heard he was a micromanager.*	*Might he get someone to mentor him on how to delegate early and often?*

IV. Actively Grow and Marshall Your Network

How do you find these people who meet the criteria and should be part of your network? The answer is simple: go where people are, look and listen, and meet and greet until you find the right people, those with the expertise and sense of collegiality you need.

When I say "go where the right people are," I'm thinking in particular of three geographies: social media, events and conferences, and organizational hierarchies.

To begin with, this is an age of active social media networks, in which professional groups have developed online networks to supplement and complement the real-life networks that guide their thinking and real-time decisions. Do you know who is most influential in your network of peers and clients? Only by identifying those people can you target them for outreach. Even if such people may not proactively take steps to help you, they may talk about you, so you want to make sure you're proactively talking to them and are helpful to them.

That's why it is so important to be on Twitter, Facebook, and professional sites and to go to key events. Those are the places where you can identify the people others ask for advice, or see who gets the most "Likes," or notice the folks people make sure they say hello to. You should also check Klout—and similar social media analytics sites—to monitor who is influential in an industry or discipline. Similarly, a search on LinkedIn lets you see who shows up when you search for your product space and in your geography. Make a note and watch what they comment on. These are the people you want to follow.

You also want to cultivate a broad network across divisions and up and down the hierarchy; such a network within the organization is essential when you need to exchange ideas and rally collaborative support. Maintaining an internal network and a Rolodex of intra-organizational contacts that extends well beyond your own work unit means that when you are ready, you can send your ideas throughout the organization and be sure you will be heard. Do you routinely check in with leaders you have met to find out what's on their minds and how you might go beyond your current job to help them do theirs?

By the same token, do you promote collaboration and remove obstacles to teamwork across the organization? The us-against-them mentality when talking about other divisions is both foolish and self-defeating. Instead, do you invite representatives from other divisions into your team meeting in order to share what you are learning from your clients? You should.

Do you regularly and openly acknowledge the individuals on your team? Apart from the effect this is likely to have on their work, they may advance to other parts of the organization and can be connectors for you in the future.

Finally, keep a networking mindset always. I discovered an app called Timehop, which reminds you of what you were thinking of in previous years; that is, two years ago, five years ago, and so on. It does this by pointing you to your tweets or Facebook mentions in past years. I've found it to be a helpful tool. When one of the Timehop reminders reminds me of something I may have mentioned that is relevant to a friend or client, I bounce it on via an e-mail to them with a hello. Inevitably, the recipient is delighted to hear from me and to re-engage about the issue at hand. So, that is an example of a simple, "huh, fun" app that I was able to turn into a networking tool. Think about other things in your environment—events, alumni parties, article alerts—that you can use as a way to connect with people around real content.

Checkpoint: Day in the Life of Networkers

If you can, try some best practice observations. Catalogue a "day in the life" of the top-performing peer or team member who seems to get the best out of their network.

This can reveal the often unconscious practices that work best in your specific company and customer/market environment, and set top performers apart from their peers. For example, best practice observations in a mid-sized software firm recently revealed that top-performing sales teams created significantly more and higher value added meetings by using their technical teams directly with their customers. These result in longer-term, more profitable customer relationships. Their interactions with the technical team were not especially difficult to document and replicate across other sales teams, and resulted in real revenue impact in the first few years.

Let's now create your plan for reaching out to the people and groups you want to connect with (identified earlier in step 2). How will you connect with them?

Table 4.6
James' Network Plan

Person or group	Social media	Events and conferences	Organizational hierarchies
Example: James would like to meet MIT Media Lab leads, over meaning-ful work.	He follows the key Twitter accounts of the obvious MIT Media Lab contacts, but also those who follow relevant hashtags.	James targets MIT Media Lab open houses.	James also asks the CEO for an introduction to specific leaders who are happy to return the call.

V. Provocatively Engage Your Network as the Honest Outsider

For years, I've been thinking about the role of the honest outsider in holding the mirror up to organizations. One of my first non-consulting roles emerged because of a casual discussion during a social brunch with a senior banking executive in which I laid out all the ways his bank had lost the opportunity to have me as a client. I'd walked into the branch near my work during lunch in my natty suit. Five employees barely glanced at me as they put up signs around the bank or generally hung around. I picked up the high-net worth brochure, reviewed it, and stared meaningfully at the teller. Nobody approached me. I left, and considered the six to seven opportunities they'd missed to engage me. This discussion resulted in him asking me to join his operations, even though I'd been angling to do some consulting for the company!

Some recent news events reminded me of that event as well as watching *The League of Denial*, the PBS documentary on American football that came out in 2013, and the 2015 movie *Concussion*, which builds on the central character, Dr. Omalu.

It was Dr. Bennet Omalu who first identified the traumatic brain condition that is commonplace among American football players: CTE. The forensic pathologist conducted the autopsy of Pittsburgh Steelers center Mike Webster in 2002 after Webster died of a heart attack at 50.

Omalu is a Nigerian by birth who knew little about American football as a game; he didn't watch it even though he lived in a football-crazy city, and he didn't know anything about the legendary Webster. All he knew was that he was conducting the autopsy of a 50-year-old man whose brain showed the wear and tear of a 75-year-old. The game had battered his body, but even more, his brain. In his role as a neuropathologist, he discovered the kind of a trauma he'd never have expected—a condition called chronic traumatic encephalopathy, or CTE. The condition causes depression, memory loss, and sometimes dementia.

Omalu's lack of reverence for the player meant that he was respectful, caring, persistent, thoughtful, and ultimately absolutely the right person to work on Webster. He served Webster and his family in ways no fan ever did. He discovered the truth behind Webster's tragic last years of pain and suffering and showed that it was the disease, not the man, that was flawed.

The documentary talks about the shameful way the NFL went after Omalu, destroying his reputation and cutting him off at each turn. The truth will out, though, and in this case Omalu's persistence and integrity means that the young children going into the sport today will be protected to some extent from the myopia of the NFL, which is finally trying to change the rules of the game to make head trauma less of a possibility.

What can you learn from such outsiders in engaging with your network?

- When you engage with influential leaders in your network, share some facts that will help them recognize the deeply held beliefs of their organization that may benefit from a review once in a while. Because they support the status-quo, they may also be preventing their evolution.
  - Are there blind spots that bear closer examination?
  - Are there opportunities for growth that will protect them and their people, or grow them in ways that make you better able to succeed as the world evolves around you?
- Work with finesse:
  - In most cases, you will be taking on powerful interests, so show them that you're doing it because of your interest in their well-being and that you're coming in with integrity.

- Listen, engage, test, and decide thoughtfully how you construct your insights.
- Engage constructively. Use phrases such as "How can we test if that is really the case?" and fewer "but" or "I know" ones.
- Maybe help them design a method for testing your insight, even if it's as simple as focus grouping the question with your team or a small group of their own employees.

- Recognize that you are part of a change process. Know that you will not be popular.
- Be truthful. You may not be a data wonk, but establish and communicate your approach. My own experience has been that there's only so much data you can collect, and people who do not want to be convinced won't be, so capture enough information and data, and then make sure you communicate it thoughtfully.
- Examine your own motivations. If there is any self-interest involved, either

remove that motivation or be absolutely transparent about it. That way, it's clear to everyone where you are coming from.

- Above all else, understand the others' point of view, which is often the status quo. Chances are, you won't agree with it anyway, but it's good to understand where the rest of them are coming from.

- Work with an empathetic insider, if you can. In most organizations, there are respected influencers who have the long-term well-being of the company at heart. If you can find and work with them, you'll be helping the change process along significantly. In Omalu's case, his cause was moved forward significantly by the doctor the NFL granted access to, Dr. Ann McKee, a self-confessed Steelers fan.

Remember, these kinds of constructive conversations can come with opportunities and action commitments, so go in ready to commit to prototyping. It can be quite exhilarating!

Now that you have a sense of your network's current strengths, possibilities, and priorities, start acting on them. Learn from the people in your network; be open-hearted with them so they value you as much as you value them and so that you can activate your Rolodex to learn and grow!

Checkpoint: For the Parents Reading This Book

A majority of our innovator interviews pointed to the role of parents in the nurturing and engagement of their unique mindsets and abilities. Parents often accepted the uniqueness of these children, even when they were inconvenient or outside of the norms. An engineering leading light who grew up in Minnesota talked about how they didn't push him to conform in any way, even indulging his requests for mail-order catalogues for computer parts when they were a rare commodity. He'd found his first love! You'll read about Rado Kotorov in Chapter 6. A polymath and innovator, Rado talked about his family prizing learning above all other things, including while at the dinner table, even as the communist state closed down much deep inquiry in public forums.

Our survey showed some interesting insights. Almost 70 percent of respondents credited parents and their upbringing for their innovation abilities.

Inclusive behaviors, exposing children to new ideas in family settings, resisting the urge to get the child to specialize (unless they wanted to), and being a partner rather than a rule-setter seem to be the key characteristics we can identify of these parents. It's worth thinking about as you nurture your young'uns.

CHAPTER 5

Discipline #4: Prototype the Possibilities

Patrick (a composite of clients) stopped me at the end of one of my talks at a TiE (The Indus Entrepreneurs, a global organization of entrepreneurs and angel investors) event a couple of years ago while traveling in Europe. He was intrigued by the Harvard research I had shared on how men tended to be more confident about their capabilities than women when it came to applying to jobs where they had only some of the experiences listed in the job description. He wondered if he was an outlier. Once a high flyer in the energy business, with a history of developing internal start-ups, he now found himself shunted into one meaningless role after the other. The pay was just high enough to keep him shackled, and his past connections with the CEO who he'd reported to kept him in the company. But now in his mid-40s, he was in a holding pattern, seeing other hot-shots fly past him on promotions, and in one case, aggressively taking over an internal start-up he had created. What was he doing wrong?

The more we discussed his predicament, the clearer it became. Here was a "nice guy" with true technology insights that he shared freely, who had become the victim of internal politics. Here also was a guy who had lost his way. A true trail-blazer, he had been seduced by the paycheck and the corporate comfort of 10 years in the system and no longer felt he could break out of his pattern.

Sound familiar?

As Patrick and I worked together, on WebEx coaching sessions across time zones, we unearthed a series of great ideas that he'd squirreled away for the future. As we played out the possibilities, I had him write short essays in the form of e-mails to me. In each case he would describe a future in which he had played out one of his ideas or inventions. In each call he would ask if he really wanted to leave "a good job and paycheck" for the wide unknown. I'd urge him to tell me why the paycheck felt good, and whether he really felt the job was good, given the description he often gave me of the daily slights he had to endure. At the end of these sessions, he would write a transcendent piece, describing in deep detail a future where he had taken control in some way and truly begun to live up to his potential. After a few of these write-ups, a pattern began to emerge. He inevitably described belonging to a company that was a true meritocracy, and he would have developed a technology platform that he could take globally. A particular focus was a tech-based platform. As he clarified his vision, he slowly pulled together a team—he's just looking for the right time to pounce now. What was the real difference between the Patrick of December 2015 and April 2016? Many things: he had developed a financial plan that laid out his liabilities and possibilities, he had realistically set out his capabilities and understood what differentiated him, and he had activated his network with a vengeance. But, most importantly, he had prototyped his new venture and his life. He had begun to visualize a different future. As he played out the possibilities, he began to act on them.

I first learned about visualization when playing sports. Rifle-shooting competitions are long marathons. You set up, take a few sighting shots, and then have to shoot 60 shots, ideally right through the center of the target. When I was shooting competitively, you had between an hour and two to shoot the competition. In that time, all kinds of issues would come into play: different wind and light conditions, fatigue, and distractions related to each new shooting range the competition was being held in. When traveling, you often had only a day or two of practice in the range. In my case, I was also playing a rather expensive sport, coming from a country and background which had limited resources to spare. So, while my competitors would have days of shooting hundreds of shots, my coach guided me to play out each shot in my mind multiple times in multiple conditions. After a day of shooting, I would sit back and play out a few matches in my head and in each case would try and feel each muscle at work, and the interplays of light, shade, and wind.

This same practice came handy for me as I made the shift from being a provincial student from southern India to studying in Oxford and then on to working in the Big Apple. Mapping out the myriad unknowns didn't fully account for all the curve-balls that life threw, but it certainly helped me see the possibilities as I walked into new arenas.

My "worst" client, as he puts it, is Sree Sreenivasan, my husband (@Sree on Twitter). When I met him in 1999, he was well set to be a lifer at Columbia University, where he was a pro-fessor at the Journalism School. In our first nine years together, though, he began a redesign of his capabilities. Even as he taught at the Journalism School, he rapidly developed a practice around social media. At a time when people complained about how Twitter and Facebook were a space for sharing photos of lunch, he was exploring how businesses and leaders could use these platforms to build new capabilities, showcase expertise, and drive a fan following.

Just as I was convinced that he was set to be an academic for life, he began exploring the idea of MOOCs, "massive open online courses," and how Columbia University might develop a response to them. In essence, he created his new job, the chief digital officer (CDO) role at Columbia.

Now imagine my surprise when he decided in 2013 to leave the institution he'd worked at for 20 years. He'd had a lifelong admiration for the Metropolitan Museum of New York, and jumped at the chance to be CDO there. I went along, with some misgivings . . . and three years later, my worst fears came to pass. The institution, mired in financial setbacks, decided to ramp back to basics rather than be future-focused. Despite having introduced new audiences to the power and relevance of the Met and helped redefine what digital means to museums, he and a series of digital-first leaders were let go. In those three years, he had transformed the Met, having led the delivery of the unique Met App, #MetKids, The Artist Project, and Facebook 360 immersive videos. He had revitalized the MetLab. Overnight, this legacy was set aside. Rather than collapse into himself, Sree, who was seen as a godfather of social media, decided to "social" this crisis out. He knew that, at his level, straight-out job offers would take a while to design. So the same day the Met sent a company-wide memo about his departure, he went ahead and posted a heartfelt note on Facebook. He'd of course shared it with loved ones and good friends. He proceeded to design a vision of his future self during one week that encompassed all his skills, his network, and his passions. Rather than jumping into the next big job, he established a consultancy based on the generous outreach of friends and their contacts. At the time of writing this book, Sree is the CDO of New York City, having actively redesigned his future, rapidly prototyping with conviction.

Let's explore how you can put together what you have learned about your current self and the trends that might shape the context of your work life right now. Ask yourself what kinds of jolts are valid for you.

Checkpoint: Survey Insights

A significant majority (74 percent) of respondents who generate new ideas say that they almost always "finish things despite obstacles."

Perseverance is a trait that innovators have in common. Challenges exist in every career path; overcoming these obstacles is not easy and not every obstacle is worth tackling. However, if you put in the effort to test the possibilities and refine your career vision, you can create a truly innovative path for yourself.

To answer that question, you will first need to challenge your own assumptions in several key spaces. What are your assumptions—what do you "know" to be true—about what you are willing to give up and what you are willing to take on, about what customers or employers want in terms of products or services, and about when they want it and how you can serve them? Once you have clearly set forth your assumptions in each of these spaces, you'll proceed to turn the assumptions on their heads by answering four key "what if" questions.

1. Your personal equation: What if you changed what you are willing to do, what you are willing to give up, and what you are willing to take on?

2. What: What if the customers and/or employers want a whole other experience?

3. When: What if they could access these services (or products) at another time?
4. How: What if they were willing to be serviced another way?

The results will be surprising and will likely prompt you to reframe your vision of yourself, think bigger, and expand your options as you reaffirm the soundness of the jolt you want to undertake.

Based on these freeing questions, I ask you to imagine throwing yourself into a video game—Minecraft, to take a ubiquitous example. You are suddenly in a different world. The very first thing you do is look around to see what's there and what tools and mechanisms you can use to create a home. Picture your whole new future in viscerally clear, videogame terms and look around. Do you feel and can you see how and where to begin and what specific tools or mechanisms will be required? In this chapter, I will guide you in crafting the story of yourself as a few different avatars in different career trajectories so you can taste each and find which feels like home and fits your natural self.

Markets, trends, consumers, products, technology, and world events all have one thing in common:

they don't stand still, and neither can one's planning for the next jolt. It means you must stay attuned to shifts—both dramatic and subtle—so that you are poised continually to jolt your work life. All the tasks of personally managing one's career require that one remain alert and mentally limber, able to shift gears quickly and in the right direction for the plan.

This chapter discusses the three strategies for doing so:

I. Bottle serendipity: Keep your mind open to serendipity so you catch the signals that both the external and internal worlds send to them.

II. Always a design mind: Invest in understanding the basics and use some of the elements of design thinking in your life.

III. Career-focused rapid prototyping: How can you bring the spirit of rapid prototyping while still bringing one's whole self to work? It's about strategically compartmentalizing the experiments and the day-to-day and combining them to test for the next level possibilities.

I. Bottle Serendipity

When I first moved to New York City 16 years ago, I only knew the colleagues at the consulting firm I was recruited into. They were a fun crew, and weekday evenings were pretty well taken care of with late evenings at work and team dinners. The weekends were a little more of a challenge. Of course, New York has no dearth of activities and programs. It's really more about making the choice of what to do among the myriad opportunities.

That's when I came up with a strategy that I continue to this day when I am in an unfamiliar city or find myself at a loose end. It's a way of capturing serendipity. I'd take the subway to a neighborhood I'd wanted to explore. Getting out of the subway station, I'd walk to the nearest traffic lights and then let the algorithm of the lights guide me. I'd take whichever green light came up, turning to make sure I wasn't waiting at any point. Inevitably, I'd find a museum, art gallery, park, show, place to eat, or some hidden gem that would eat up the rest of my day. In a couple of weeks, I felt like I knew Manhattan: Harlem, Soho, the Upper East Side, Central Park, the Upper West Side, and Brooklyn.

I've done this in Paris, Istanbul, and London and never regretted it!

It often reminded me of the meandering route I take with the Sunday newspapers. Rather than finishing a section, I find myself following the "Turn to page . . ." approach to guide my reading. Once I move to a new section and finish the story, I move to the next article in that section. It's lots of fun and works online too, I'm sure.

Take Action: Manufacture Serendipity

Whether it's walking around a city or navigating life in general, try something new because it's presented to you serendipitously. This can be a fun way to mix up your routine and open yourself up to new ways of thinking and being. Here are a few exercises to try, perhaps one a week or one a month (preferably on the first of each month). I recommend starting with a planned approach, because it's a good way to get yourself into a rhythm. As you get into the habit, you won't need a calendar.

- If you find yourself with a couple of hours on a weekend, flip through the newspapers or online to the first show in town and see if you can get out to see it, even if you normally wouldn't go.

- Get onto local Websites or those like Eventbrite and see if there's a conference in town that you can walk through to get the flavor of a new industry.
- If you're on online platforms like Twitter, look out for Twitter Chats and join in the conversation around a new space. Or select Twitter's "Moments" section and see if there are stories you know nothing about to learn more.
- Do you live in a university town or anywhere near a university? Check if there are lectures you can sit in on; there are often visiting speakers that have open sessions to the public.
- Do a simple walkabout in the city. Walk through galleries, find hackathons in motion, or find hidden museums.

Bon chance!

Careers and industries are shifting with almost quantum speed. Roles and industries that were prestigious are beleaguered, and some no longer exist. Jobs rise and fall. The chief innovation officer came and went in the 2000s; the chief digital offi-cer role is watched closely, having come to be in the early 2010s, but is now often getting folded into the chief marketing officer role.

Similarly, cutting-edge technologies rise, lan-guish, and fall. Bitcoin and blockchain technologies have risen into prominence since the develop-ment of bitcoin in 2008. However, eminent bitcoin developers have left the ecosystem recently, and significant losses due to cyber-attacks have shaken the foundations of this cyber economy. Even less technical innovations like the ubiquitous Web por-tals of the 2000s or the app economy begin to play less focal roles within years of rising to prominence.

At this pace, how do you craft long-term plans? Well, you don't. Be open to serendipity. As new technologies, opportunities, or pathways emerge before you, take advantage of them and follow them to see where they lead. This can be done even as you stay in your current role.

The number of examples of how serendipity helped drive the direction of innovators' lives is staggering. Let's take one eminent example.

Leila Janah had done her graduate studies and research in development studies at Harvard, then at Ashoka and the World Bank. A combination of serendipity (right place, right time) and her drive to do more had her joining me on a project with an Indian outsourcing company. As she dug into the details and operations of outsourcing, she designed a unique operation that crafted a development-oriented double bottom-line enterprise that aimed to alleviate worldwide poverty by connecting unemployed people in impoverished countries to digital work. One of the first organizations to engage in impact sourcing, Samasource uses an Internet-based model called "microwork" to break down large-scale digital projects from clients into smaller tasks for workers to complete. These workers are trained in basic computer skills and paid a fair wage.

How did Leila's story evolve?

Leila first went to Africa at 17, funded mostly by a scholarship she had impulsively signed up for as she sat in the high school counselor's office. The $10,000 fund allowed her to get a break from a household where tensions ran high—this was just meant to be her escape for the summer. Her family hadn't the funds to send her off to Ghana, but she'd found a way to get herself out there. She hauled off to Ghana and spent the second semester of her senior year in high school teaching English to blind students. She learned Braille, and developed a curriculum from the U.S. embassy library. Here she was developing a creative writing program for students who were just starving for opportunity and information. They tried so hard, undeterred by their handicap. Leila talks about how her experience that term shifted everything she imagined she knew about poverty, including the oft-stated truisms that poor people are poor because of lack of work ethic, hard-working mind-set, or values. What she was experiencing was that people had to work tremendously hard in places like Ghana then to just survive.

Her passion for battling global poverty had been ignited. How could people who were so talented be so poor? How could they die because they couldn't have a five dollar vaccination? Time and time again, she found that what people wanted was not charity, but work.

On her return, Leila decided she'd find ways to keep going back. She worked a series of part-time jobs as she studied—legal secretary, SAT tutoring, janitorial service, ticket sales—and these funded her trips back to work with a series of nonprofits.

As she says, "Working my butt off forced me to get beyond the trust fund charity mindset." Leila went on to graduate in African development studies at Harvard. She took on grants and internships to fund trips back to Africa. Her realization from her discussions with the recipients of the services of NGOs (non-governmental organizations) was that they really didn't need more legal scholars telling them they need better legal systems—they needed jobs. They needed investments to fuel growth, not the paternalistic or academic mind-set then prevalent in the view to growing Africa.

She delved deep into the entrepreneurial approach, interning for Ashoka (the non-profit focused on developing innovators and entrepreneurs) in India. She got the chance to spend time with social entrepreneurs in India dealing with tough issues and developing innovative solutions with, for example, the group that organized slum children who were already collecting trash, helping them unionize and get contracts with cities.

Then came the moment of serendipity. She had joined Katzenbach Partners when she graduated from Harvard, aiming to develop her business skills. It just so happened that I had sold a piece of work with an outsourcing company in India. It wasn't an easy project to staff. We were looking at a lot of travel to India, and with a slim team that would have little backup support because we weren't charging top dollar given exchange rates. Given her Indian heritage, this Californian decided to give it a shot and got on a plane to come with me to Mumbai.

Leila warned me that she knew little about business and less about outsourcing. I explained that consulting was often about asking the transformational questions, learning deep and fast, and engaging fearlessly. "I found that so helpful in battling the imposter syndrome. Seeing you stride into rooms full of men in a largely paternalistic society, and be listened to was eye-opening," said Leila. Within weeks, we were chest-high in the operational details of a leading consulting firm.

Apropos our chapter on stalking trends, Leila began to put the pieces together. She had already been intrigued by the idea of micro-finance, having read the works of Muhammad Yunus, founder of the Grameen Bank. She began to see how she might put that concept together with outsourcing. In addition, we were all feeling the practical impact of globalization on a daily basis. Americans were buying things and services made elsewhere in places like Bangladesh. How could we disavow responsibility for the makers, when we were using the fruits of their labor?

The ideas were percolating in her mind when she took a summer break with friends in Kenya. She happened to have a dinner-time conversation with a dean of the University of Kenya about how she might make her concept work there. Kenya was at that time dealing with a 20 percent unemployment rate among its educated urban population. They homed in on the Internet cafes of Kenya. Computers often sat idle, as the price per minute of online access was pretty steep. She set out to get a network of Internet cafe owners together and shared her vision. If they could recruit hard working, smart, and technically savvy but truly poor folks, she would find work for them. The die was cast and she returned to the United States on a mission. She started by winning a contract from a non-profit in Palo Alto called Book Share for a data entry project. In the coming years, that first $30,000 of contract revenue turned to $250,000 in revenue.

Leila had built on her knowledge (development and law), assets (a deep network), and capabilities (strategy and business development) and used a serendipitous discovery (outsourcing) to create a whole new endeavor. Sama Group, Leila's first company, has had backers as eminent as Richard Branson and now employs 1,500 people around the world. They use technology and private sector methods in new ways to measurably improve poor people's access to dignified work, critical medical care, and education. Since 2008, the Sama Group has grown three successful social enterprises and helped cultivate a new industry, impact sourcing.

As Leila sees it, "You can plan all you want—you can make all kinds of plans—in reality, any success you see is due to you being open to change and being prepared. Now I have the capabilities and team to swing into action when opportunities arise."

This "bottling of serendipity" can work in much less dramatic ways as well, from the sublime to the more mundane. When I was at Pfizer in the early 2000s, I watched blogging and microblogging coming to the fore. I knew I wanted to test-drive this democratic publishing trend, but I couldn't blog about anything I was a professional expert at. I was in strategy roles and anything I revealed would in some ways reflect what Pfizer was considering or developing. I realized I could develop my blogging experience by blogging about something I enjoyed. I had just started introducing my kids to cooking, so I began blogging recipes and about experiences working with the kids in the kitchen. Before too long, I had a recipe blog with more than 100 recipes and more than 100,000 page views. I've had people suggest I publish a cook book. I've been tempted.

II. Always a Design Mind

Although conventional design thinking begins at observation and the well-crafted question, brainstorming, and then selection, innovators seems to have an almost constant combination and question machine running in the background. One of the innovators interviewed described it as a constant casino slot machine—rotating through issues, ideas, and insights.

Listening to a start-up founder working to develop a sustainability stamp of approval in the entertainment industry, we heard the mutual tumblers going in our heads: how does an unknown start-up become the arbiter of standards? In the entertainment industry, it was about taking the core of the industry—film festivals—and launching a stamp that brought together all sustainable programming wherein they fast-tracked the development of a common stamp of approval.

Innovators tend to overwhelmingly see the innovation as a complex culmination of putting together a jigsaw puzzle of all the conventional drivers: new products, new services, new ways of sharing or accessing information, and changing existing products and services. Non-ideators, or those who describe themselves as more focused on execution than innovation, tend to define innovation more in terms of products and services. The jigsaw puzzle mentality allows for greater flexibility and ability to craft unique options.

One way to make this jigsaw puzzle happen is to ask the right questions more consistently. At the core, design thinking is about asking highly effective questions about a few key elements. In product design, the questions can go like this:

- What is the current experience for the customer?

- How, when, and why do they use this product or service?
- What if we changed one or many of these factors (what, how, when, and why they use it)?
- What's exciting about that change?
- What's good about that change?
- How is the customer's experience measurably different?

III. Career-Focused Rapid Prototyping

Most of those reading this book probably have a current job, or feel like they are on a specific track. So how do you get the catapult ready, while still maintaining the current?

It's a version of rapid prototyping. Companies sometimes need to establish new products, while continuing to extract value from their existing products. Think of this in a similar way.

Rippan Kapur was an airline purser who lived in India. He's seen children in slums beg, and he was often struck by the folks he worked with in the airlines. He reacted viscerally to the contrasts: seeing children begging and working as servants or laborers around Indian cities and villages. In 1979, even as he worked as a purser, he began an experiment and asked passengers if they had foreign coins to contribute, specifically, Indian coins, on their flights out to their hometowns. This was one of his early experiments. This young man brought together like-minded friends and, while still in his mid-20s, worked with six of them to engage on how they could make this a sustained effort. Instead of starting a grassroots-level organization working directly with underprivileged children, Kapur and his friends opted to create an organization that would be a link between the millions of Indians with resources, and the thousands of dedicated individuals and organizations at the grassroots level struggling to function for lack of them. In the 1970s, this was a new idea. They then took it one step further. Child Rights and You (CRY) would become one of the early examples of a social enterprise. Their early efforts were funded by the sale of curated, high-end cards and stationary that they advertised with clear messages on the impact of such change.[1]

Although the story of his collecting of coins during flights is anecdotal, this was a man who packed a lot into his young life. The coin experiment probably inspired the UN "Change for Good" program that now collects change from multiple global airlines. Rippan died at the age of 40. Here was someone who started with an idea discussed around his mother's dining table with six friends and 50 rupees (roughly $1 at the time of this writing). He then set off to experiment with other ways to work rather than just giving a hand-out. He used his insights from flights and engaging with the people he met at work to understand the spirit and design aesthetic of those he might tap into to fund his vision. Here was someone who did use the insights of his current work to test and evolve his vision to create an organization that has brought education, health, and support to hundreds of thousands of children in India.

Rapid Prototyping

In engineering, rapid prototyping is a group of techniques used to quickly fabricate a scale model of a product using 3D computer-aided design (CAD) data. In many ways, it builds on the work of the ancients. For example, think of the images and models that Leonardo da Vinci created. In essence, you get a sensory feel of your product or offering without breaking the bank. You work out the kinks, and then go into production when you feel like the design is done and the functionality you want to deliver is right there. With the advent of 3D printing, this area is opening up like never before.

The core techniques or idea behind rapid prototyping is quickly repeating cycles of creation, review, and revision, to get from an idea to a working product as quickly as possible.

Prototyping can take many forms. In engineering, the "low-fidelity" model is to simply draw something out, and the high-fidelity model is to create a working prototype.

In da Vinci's world, that would be the evolution from his sketches to his detailed drawings of plans to the test prototypes he made and in some cases tested such as, for example, the aerial screw helicopter he designed but probably never fully tested.

In engineering, this process would include a sketch, then a wire frame, and then a minimum viable product or app.

Take Action: Career Rapid Prototyping

What does it mean in the case of the career catapult? Build on the exercise in design thinking here.

- Low fidelity: If you are a visual person, you can literally sketch this out; but if not, you could frame it as answers to three simple questions:
  - What does my making this change look like? What will be different about me and my world?
  - What will it feel like? How will this make me feel about the work I do?
  - What changes in the output of my work? At the end of each day, week, month, or year, what will I measure myself against?
- Medium fidelity: Now write this out in more of an essay format. Can you visualize this?
- High fidelity: Write a short business plan or rewrite your resume to reflect all of those learnings you've been gleaning from your review.

Now Review

Talk to a few people who know the space and test out the questions on them. What does their life and work look like, feel like, and how do they measure their work? Does your business plan work? Would your new resume be on target?

Would they let you walk around their shop floor or company? Can you volunteer to help with a key initiative? Can you test your hypothesis on how the work will look, feel, and be measured?

Refine

Based on your insights from those conversations, get back to the drawing board and keep refining your low, medium, and high-fidelity vision of your next step.

Open your mind and heart to the serendipity of insights. Take the time to understand the drivers for your design. Work diligently to prototype your vision and create a few options. Leila's path to Sama Group took years, but it was a magical journey. Yours can be too.

CHAPTER 6

Discipline #5:
Go Extreme!

What can the disruption look like for you? It should feel like home. Make sure you have the time, the energy, the money, the contacts, and the fire in the belly to make it happen.

So far, we've discussed how you can dig deep to understand your drivers, strengths, and blind spots; how you can stalk trends to start identifying your leverage point to catapult into a new future; and you've activated your network and begun to prototype your possibilities. Now it's time to go extreme.

As I mentioned in the previous chapter, I have the good fortune of being right beside someone who truly believes in "going extreme": Sree.

My husband, Sree Sreenivasan, joined Columbia University right after he finished his master's degree at the Journalism School. For the first dozen years of our marriage he had been a university employee—first as a professor of New Media Journalism, then an associate dean of the Journalism School. With time, he'd built out his experience on a foundation of technology reporting to truly becoming a leading authority on all things social and digital. He moved into the role of chief digital officer (CDO) of Columbia. He'd also built out his social presence but had imbued those platforms with his personal charm and helpfulness. So, when New York's Metropolitan Museum of Art hired him as its first-ever CDO in 2013, that move made headlines. Sree's remit was to connect the world to the treasure trove that was the Met. He took over a 70-person team that created the museum's first app, refreshed the extensive Website, developed deeply engaging visual content, and revitalized its Media Lab.

The #EmptyMet Story

I remember him turning to me at the end of his first day of work, and saying how amazing it was to walk through the hallowed halls of the Met early in the morning, with not another soul in sight. The museum opens to the public at 10 a.m., and so as he walked in at 8 a.m. for the next few weeks, alone apart from the guards and the janitors checking on the lights and floors, he shared the gems on Twitter, Instagram, and Facebook. As people started commenting on those posts, about how lucky he was to have this opportunity, he started building on a hashtag that had been used by other employees: #EmptyMet.

During the next few months, Sree developed a personal tour on which he would take small groups of friends, social media influencers, and real-world influencers, distilling for them the excitement he felt for this fabulous institution and the art it held. Through the next couple of years, hundreds of folks and celebrities from around the world went on #EmptyMet tours. In the spring of 2016, to celebrate Facebook founder Mark Zuckerberg's fourth wedding anniversary, his staff worked with Sree to arrange an #EmptyMet tour for Zuckerberg and his wife Priscilla Chan. The Met developed a business version of the tours and now offers #EmptyMet tours to the public.

Along the way, Sree was named to *Fast Company*'s list of the 100 Most Creative People in Business, for a wide range of initiatives and projects. The magazine credited Sree with "liberating the museum from its physical walls."[1]

So, when the Met suddenly told Sree that he'd have to leave the organization as part of a broader cost-cutting move, he and I were befuddled. Here was a guy who had done so much to bring new kinds of attention to the Met and who truly loved his job being asked to move on.

#Sree3oh

Most executives would have opted for the "spending time with family" line or withdrawing from the public eye. After a weekend in a shocked daze, Sree bounced back, and boy was that a sight to behold!

In a few days, when the news became public, Sree posted a note on Facebook.

The spirit of the message was gratitude and adventure. He shared the Met's departure memo, and then launched what he called Sree 3.0 (1.0 was his 21 years at Columbia, 2.0 was his three years at the Met). He would take on speaking engagements, consult, write a book, and yes, take time for a family vacation in India. He also invited all his friends to sign up for a walk with him (he walks around 5–7 miles a day) and share their insights on what he should do as a next step via a Google form. As many as 1,300 people responded to his query. The suggestions went from the funny (running for President as an alternative to Trump and Clinton) to a job idea our children loved (being the CDO of Nutella).

The comments on his Facebook post were supportive and constructive. High-powered executives recommended him to even more influential folks. Walks in the park with him turned into walking brainstorms with important media folks.

This was a whole new twist to being laid off— Fired 3.0!

And he kept sharing: explaining all the opportunities he was exploring, and sharing ways to relax into the realities of this new phase in his life. *Quartz* published a profile with this headline: "The Met ousted a top executive, so he used Facebook to show the world how to do unemployment right."[2]

When, a month into his unemployment, Sree was able to announce that he'd been appointed CDO of New York City by Mayor Bill de Blasio, the digirati went wild, with messages of support coming from all around the world.

So what did the Sreexit (a reference to the Brexit vote when Britain exited the European Union at the same time and coined by Indian politician and writer Shashi Tharoor) illustrate?

- Sree had spent his early years learning about the digital space and he'd built out his people management skills along the way.
- When most people had dismissed social media platforms as "ways to talk about their breakfast," Sree had watched and engaged deeply on all platforms and was one of the early CDOs who emerged from the space.
- He'd built an active community, help-ing others along the way for decades. So, when he had a need, that network jumped right in to help him.
- He's always engaged in the world of nonprofits and public programs. So, in

a way, he'd been prepping for the New York City CDO job for 20 years, not just applying in the weeks prior to the appointment!

Faced with a first-in-a-lifetime situation of being fired, Sree chose to go extreme. He amped up the volume on gratitude, transparency, and asking for help!

This is a pattern you can see around you, if you look hard enough. Inevitably, whenever there is the option to take a baby step, innovators seem to take a deep breath and think about what the extreme or big option is—and then they take it. It's not about wanton risk-taking, either. It's about taking a clear-eyed view of the options and choosing to make the choice count.

Rado Kotorov grew up in Soviet-era Bulgaria. He remembers the time before the Iron Curtain fell; the limitations of that era were in many ways also the basis of certainty. When the curtain fell, there was freedom as well as all kinds of associated ambiguities and uncertainties. To someone like Rado, that meant also a series of opportunities. He had been a law student, as law was one of the freest or perhaps least restricted professions and the closest job to freelancing at that time. But he'd always been interested in business. He'd actively participated in the process of liberation from the iron yoke, so when the opportunity presented itself, he took it. As he described it, "Rather than the blacks and whites of the past, I realized I could color in the grey."

Rado looked within himself and beyond; he knew that he wanted to read more than he'd had access to before. He wanted to learn languages and read the old classics that had been banned under the communist regime. How would he solve for that? Publishing would be the key. Decades of restrictions seemed to prevent a free publishing industry, but Rado and two of his contacts used his legal brain and found a loop hole in the law. They went to court and earned the right to set up Bulgaria's first independent publishing house. So there he was, at 24, a bona fide publisher. From selling his books out of car trunks, he went on to create a viable and successful company.

Serendipity again raises its beautiful head. He credits part of his success with his publishing endeavor with his books being very visible on the coffee table of the future prime minister, Dimitar

Iliev Popov. A judge, who went on to become Bulgaria's first noncommunist leader, Popov's candidacy was just announced and the TV channels went to interview him in his house. A set of four books on the history of the Macedonian movement for independence from Turkey were on his coffee table. So when they asked him what he was reading, he just pointed to them. Rado's partner, the lawyer Konstantin Simeonov had coincidentally given the books to him the day before. Popov probably hadn't read them as yet, but this coincidence put the books on TV. They were now on the reading list of the future prime minister! This fabulous, hilarious, chance exposure would be the tipping point for his company catapulting into prominence.

In the coming years, Rado would go on to set up Bulgaria's first credit card company, get three patents in diverse areas, and unlock the imagination of a series of start-up founders he advises as the chief innovation officer of the company, Information Builders.

The early years were not easy. He'd grown up in a family where career certainty was most prized, rather than risk-taking. He remembers avoiding his mother, who spent much of her time crying as he launched his early ventures! But it was also a family that prized learning. Whether she knew it or not, mom was nurturing his curiosity and the desire to work. Rado treasures the learning experience; he pushes himself to learn something new every six months, having to relearn everything and almost "getting to earn a new degree" of sorts. This mind-set—of diving into new spaces and disciplines to learn deeply—is Rado's way of going extreme. Entrepreneurs need to have a broad grasp of legal, financial, accounting, and design disciplines. You can learn as you go, but definitely learn. He's got formal education in law, finance and marketing, a PhD in game theory, math and philosophy, and even fashion design. This is someone who truly believes in the interdisciplinary experience. If there's one thing he is concerned about today, it is the education systems' insistence on driving children to a single track too early. They lose the ability to think conceptually and can't see the forest for the trees. He credits his educational experience for his ability—critical for all entrepreneurs—to go from the ground hog view to the eagle view and back again. In other words, he has the ability to move from the details to the big picture and back.

He also credits some of his inventiveness to his early rebellion against the politics of that time. He had begun to see business as a driver of change. Europe remains conservative and is not good with failure. The United States treats failure as a learning opportunity. It's not a coincidence that Rado moved to the United States at the first opportunity.

Checkpoint: The Power of Patents and Never Giving Up

Rado reflects on what he learned from his patenting experience:

> Getting a patent teaches you a lot. Getting the first patent makes you very unrealistically hopeful. You think it will make the business big. But the failure actually teaches you humility. In our case (for the coffee machine), there was big interest from firms to license it, but then nothing happened as the market got saturated with bottled coffee drinks. So the companies felt it was a crowded market. Many inventors become angry with such situations and never invent again. They think the system is unjust—the

big guys win. But this is not true. You actually learn never to hold to an idea. The market is very dynamic, so you have to re-invent. Your next idea is always better. My patent of Active technologies, which we co-invented with Gerry Cohen, CEO of Information Builders, has been extremely successful with millions of users worldwide of the technology. Patents teach you discipline and rigor, and if you learn this and keep inventing, one of your products will be successful. So instead of stopping when the market swings another way, keep inventing.

Rado typifies the "go extreme" approach; he's not jumping out of planes, but when he sees an opportunity, he thinks about the largest possible answer. For example, when he first moved to the United States and was enabling a string of coffee shops with his analytics package, he watched the inefficiencies of the system and designed a disposable coffee press that he then patented. It's the kind of big thinking that has paid off, even if this specific invention didn't go far (or so far, at least).

Rado warns that this kind of commitment takes work and can sometimes feel frustrating.

And the early stages of growth can be chaotic. There are no three- or five-year plans. However, you can take a structured approach. This is about making the mental transition from free to structured thinking about your idea or opportunity. As Rado describes it, it's time to "get out of your jeans and sweat pants and put your suit on."

So now you've found your opportunity. In Rado's case, he knew he wanted to read and access the country's past literature and assumed others did too. Lindsay knew she wanted to be in the food and travel space.

Going extreme means taking the idea and seeing what the most imaginative and ultimate version of that idea might be, and then making it implementable.

As early as 1986, management thinkers and researchers C.K. Prahalad and Richard Bettis brought together past research and conducted their own studies about the skills that leaders of good single-business companies have as against those of multi-sector companies. They found that the ability to get beyond current assumptions was central to the leaders' ability to manage that kind of diversity and that they had to learn the ability to manage diverse businesses.[3]

Let's examine how you might proceed to think differently about your own opportunities and think extreme.

Definitely Try This at Home: Your Alchemy

As you've read this book, you have worked through critical elements of your personal alchemy by digging deep.

What have you been learning through your career and life? What are you skilled at? What blind spots have you discovered, and have you begun to address or manage them?

Who is the "you" we now have? In Sree's case, it was a social guy, with a deep sense of where the digital world was going, who can communicate fabulously about all things tech and digital to a broad, loyal network.

How do you describe yourself based on your deep review? And now, can you "supersize" yourself?

As we discussed in Chapter 2, what are the activities you perform at so consistently high a level of competency to make you competitive in the market? These are the core competencies that will be the bedrock of your expanded new horizons. Delve into them and ensure that these are capabilities that you can continue building on. You are the unique combination of your capabilities and mind-set.

Now consider what the "largest possible" version of those assets might look like. What does the best version of your expertise look like? How do you make the most of your technical capabilities? What are the specific skills you've built with time and do they set you up for taking on new opportunities? For example, when Otis, a young bank executive in charge of reporting at a Wall Street firm found himself embattled and going nowhere, we spent significant time truly engaging around why he found himself in the situation he was in. Although he was an excellent CPA, he was dealing with aggressive people who didn't want to spend time on documentation and reporting and, hence, didn't give him the time or support to help him deliver in his role. He felt stuck, until we talked through the industries where clear accounting of core assets were the key. As he made the switch to California to work in an energy start-up, this executive leveraged his deep expertise in accounting to make the shift into a new industry. This was someone who built on his core expertise to shift into a situation and geography that was much more conducive for his continued growth.

Also, consider your mind-set and orientation. In Otis's case, although he had a strong sense of personal accountability, he was not one who took on professional risk. This was someone who would deliver on his commitments every time, but knew he would only thrive in an established organization—no start-ups for him. However, his expertise and ability to develop and improve technical processes meant he liked to be in companies that needed to improve and strengthen their accounting and reporting processes.

Most interestingly, the driver for Otis to move to California was his recognition that, in many ways, his unhappiness was driven by the hard-driving and impersonal environment surrounding him in most of the institutions he'd worked at in New York.

That's when he went extreme: refining his ability to craft new processes to a fine point so he could clearly show how he had developed new accounting teams and reports, identifying whole new industries where his skills were needed, and identifying a whole new geography.

His job search had in the past been to talk to other banks. But once he *dug deep*, he focused on non-New York jobs in mid-sized companies where there was a clear need for an executive who would come and develop a strong accounting department.

Besides capabilities and mind-set, he also began to reflect on his passions. The environment and alternative energy had always drawn his attention.

Even though he'd never worked in the space, he swung for the fences. He researched the space and identified six companies he wanted to pursue. He resigned, got on a plane to San Francisco, and went knocking on doors. A couple of nail-biting months later, he was being relocated officially.

Unleash Your "New World": Leverage Trends and Your Network

Remember the "new worlds" you designed by analyzing the emerging trends you wanted to expand upon?

You've been a panther: stalking trends to see how they're shaping up, listening intently to weak signals, and combining all the new knowledge into new patterns to see what emerges.

Your network has showered you with insights and welcomed you to experience what it's like to try living in their context. You've experimented with new spaces and put yourself in networking situations that help you get a taste for emerging spaces.

What are you learning about these emerging spaces? What happens if they become the norm? For example, what if drones, autonomous cars, and neural control came together? Might we have autonomous mini flying cars that have sensors that can hear our thoughts? Now, what if you're currently a designer with a passion for materials—would you find ways to be noticed for your work with lightweight materials and spare, but classy, interior designs for small spaces?

Finding ways to communicate these big ideas consistently and often is part of how you go extreme. Being in the rooms where the future is being designed is one way. But if not, use social platforms (digital and real-world) to start both painting the picture of what your role might be in the new world, but also practicing it. Design autonomous car interiors, 3D print them, and blog about them. Connect with leaders in the field. Run local conferences and actually create a forum where this thinking will progress.

Also recognize what builds credibility in this new world. Spending time in these forums is about learning to walk the talk. Simply put, if you are trying to transition from a corporate life you only half-love to making a real difference with a social enterprise, you probably don't want to be in pin-striped suits talking about your stock options. Less extremely, if you are creating a digital plat-form, spend time learning the basics of coding. Understand the mind-set that motivates coders so they can see themselves working with you. Truly immerse yourself in the space, understand what matters in those spaces, test that you have the interest and ability to live in this space, and begin to practice living in the space. And do it big; don't go with half measures.

How Will You Bring Your New You to the World?

As this book is being written, the world is becom-ing more digital, networked, connected, shared, and intrinsically motivated. Valuations are often driven by notional concepts. When a mobile texting start-up like WhatsApp is bought by Facebook for around $20 billion, it's not because of the technology alone; it's also because of the footprint, the loyalty, and the ability to integrate into other Facebook platforms. This is a twist on the old 4Ps of marketing: product, price, promotion, and place. The place is largely virtual, but also in the palm of potentially everyone's hand; the product is not just the current product, but the potential to build on the product; the price is virtually nothing, and the promotion is negligible—truly driven by a network telling each other they need to have it.

How do you channel that spirit of change? And how will you make it extreme?

So you'd like to experiment with creating interiors for flying cars, but currently you're seeing old-fashioned leather interiors even in cars like the Tesla. What do you do? Should you take a trip out to Detroit and see if the electric car makers there might be interested in creating a whole new paradigm around space and light-weight materials? Do you go online to peer-sourcing sites to create a virtual team of materials engineers and new age transport experts to create your own start-up?

Conventionally, you'd assume that you'd have to design, manufacture, and then work on getting in-person meetings with customers (carrying a bunch of samples) to demonstrate and co-create with automobile partners.

Now reimagine that process and go extreme.

What if you engage differently? That is, what if you don't just design the interior, but design a whole new concept car? What if you can work with materials that can be 3D printed, rather than finding product manufacturers in China? Now, what if you mailed a package to a target partner with your materials cartridge and e-mailed the 3D printer design file? They plug it in and print out your designs and concepts.

That's one way to get some attention.

Take the time to push yourself to a simple framing of the story you have developed so far. Map your alchemy as Rado does in Table 6.4. You may not fill it all in one sitting, and you may need to keep working on it. Your goal should be to keep iterating until you get a sense of what you feel will fit for you.

Table 6.4
Map Your Alchemy   *Rado's Example*

Your "Alchemy"	Current	What Would the Opposite of Extreme Be?	How Will You Play?
What strengths, capabilities, and knowledge will you leverage?	*An independent-minded law student with broad interests*	*Make knowledge accessible*	*Work with literature and languages*
Trend and Network Leverage			
What are the trends and how is your network engaging with them?	*State-run publishers that are closely monitored and controlled*	*A free publishing industry that can deliver knowledge anywhere, anytime*	*Use legal skills to challenge current publishing practices*
What Products and Services?		*Language, literature, science, and other non-approved subjects*	*Start with subjects that will prepare people for the wall coming down: languages to engage with the world, literature and history, politics and the sciences*
What are the gaps in the market?	*Approved literature*		
How Are They Delivered?			
How do these products and services reach the user?	*Stores that sell government-published books*	*Anywhere, anytime*	*Self-publish and sell books from car trunk till you find other funding and sales options*

Checkpoint: Make Your Brain Your Friend

The "extreme" vision requires that you think big.

However, we are often encouraged by our culture or experiences to do exactly the opposite.

List and then mitigate five key limiters to thinking extreme and thinking big.

Crush the Imposter Syndrome

In the late 1970s and 1980s, a series of research efforts led Dr. Pauline Clance and Suzanne Ames to coin a term that has given many talented people a way to describe how they feel inside: Imposter Syndrome. It describes the sense of hollowness—the sense of being a fraud—that a surprising group wrestles with. It's surprising, because in most cases, we're talking about high achievers. Not only do they feel they're frauds, they also worry they'll get caught. Even clear successes get dismissed—it just happened, it was luck, fooled them. Clance and Ames also found that this was particularly pernicious and wide-spread among women achievers.[4]

As you plan to think extreme, make sure you nip out any imposter syndrome within you or manage it. Explicitly discuss it with your confidants and mentors. In your dig deep exercises, you will probably find that people see your accomplishments as just that—fabulous achievements. Another way is to make a list of your accomplishments. Save any positive feedback you received in performance and customer reviews and go back and relive those moments. Find an iconic symbol—a childhood medal, a piece of art you made, your child's Mother's Day or Father's Day card—something that emphasizes who you really are, rather than that negative internal voice.

Now Beats Later

Procrastination comes from all kinds of root causes: you may just not have energy, you may make excuses including not feeling prepared, or you may find the immediate pull of little things that distract you from the big things.

Recognize that you deserve a bigger future and find a way to schedule time each day or each week to prioritize this thinking and activity.

Give yourself the time and permission to prioritize this work now rather than putting it off to later.

Imperfection is Beautiful

You've heard of the 80/20 rule, right? Internalize it. You don't need to be perfect and complete to begin seeing change happen.

Let's get fancy. The 80/20 rule suggests that for many events or phenomena, 80 percent of the results or effects are driven by 20 percent of the causes or drivers. It's a version of the Pareto Principle, named after Vilfredo Pareto, an Italian economic researcher, who showed that land ownership tends to rest with 20 percent of the population, or at least did in 1890s Italy. Surprisingly, this insight came from his observations of nature, including the fact that 20 percent of his peapods contained 80 percent of the peas in his garden.

Why does this matter to you? Just remember that you don't need to limit yourself because you don't feel like you have all the information or all the time to do things perfectly. Take the Pareto approach to free yourself to imagine.

Nothing to Fear but Fear Itself—or Judgment

You don't need everyone to like, approve, or even understand your vision. You certainly don't need to worry about being judged. There are probably a small handful of people whose opinions do matter to you. Engage them. But *don't* limit yourself because of what you fear some broad group, professional peers, or social set will think of your aspirations. Hold your ideas dear, protect them, and don't give two hoots about how this broader group will judge you. Judgment comes naturally, and you can't control it, so don't even start worrying about it.

How You Talk To Yourself Matters

In the 1970s, psychologist Richard Bandler and linguist John Grinder created a process called neuro-linguistic programming (NLP) wherein they claimed that the interaction between mind and language and their interplay affects our body and behavior. Scientific research has since questioned the drivers of NLP. Although Bandler and Grinder's belief that they could transplant the mental and linguistic behaviors of successful people to others who are less successful has been challenged, there are ways to build out your own internal self-talk that can be a positive force to go extreme.

You can give yourself mental cues to steer toward the good, as psychiatrist Aaron Beck suggested with his cognitive therapy models. He too stated that thoughts, feelings, and behavior are all connected, and that individuals can move toward overcoming difficulties and meeting their goals by identifying and changing unhelpful or inaccurate thinking, problematic behavior, and distressing emotional responses.

Recognize when you get that crunch in the stomach, that hollow feeling. What was the thought that set it in motion? Work with your friends or a counselor to see if you can set that feeling aside. When your inner voice says "I can't," stop, take a breath, and think through "I can if . . . when . . . ."

Now, Time to Get Going!

Once you have done all of this, then you can hunt. Pretend you have been offered the job and think about what a week in that new state and that new position would look like. Consider what the routine of your day will look like so when you go into an interview, you can ask the questions that you need to. Don't just focus on achieving a bunch of goals, but think about how it will all work together. Imagine what your life will be like and if you'll like it. If you like to do things fast, maybe a start-up is the right place for you. If you are a thinker, maybe you should give academia or a place like Google a chance.

The last step is to "live it." Go back to your network and meet up with people in the industry to gather more information. Don't just ask them to tell you about it; have them walk you through it so you get it. Start living in the space before you start actually looking for a job in that space. For example, playing out our previous example, if you are interested in designing new interiors, look up the top five industrial engineers in your network or on LinkedIn and talk to them. Buy them lunch and ask them what keeps them up at night. That way, you can really test and be ready in a much more meaningful way for your (new) place in the sun.

CHAPTER 7

Unleash Your Disruption! The Time Is Now

Here's the secret to this book. It's not about pushing for action before you are ready. It's not about advocating change. I'm not asking you to quit, or to proactively go out and get a new job and rewrite your future. What I *am* doing is recommending that you be prepared and proactively design your careers. The strategies I suggest will bolster your change-readiness and potentially improve your own attractiveness even within your current career path and company.

One of the masters of reinvention I've had the honor of knowing is Sebastian Thrun, innovator, entrepreneur, educator, and computer scientist. He was first motivated to imagine a new way of driving by a deeply emotional event: his friend's death in an avoidable traffic accident in Germany. His mind roiled at the thought that his friend would be here but for driver error. That's when he began imagining a driverless, safe car. This wasn't about adding airbags; this was about radically redefining the idea of transport. Years later, he would engage Google's founders in the idea and help set up one of the first significant non-automobile company efforts around a transformed driving experience. Since starting the driverless car revolution, he has set out to transform other fields, including education. The idea of a massive open online course (MOOC) received a great impetus from Sebastian putting one of his Stanford University lectures online, and seeing 14,000 sign-ups during one weekend. This was the seed that has now flowered into his education start-up, Udacity. The importance of building out both the hard and soft elements of talent—the engineering, but also marketing, design, and management elements—is not lost on Sebastian.

Sebastian has set out to shift thinking about education by melding disciplines more fluidly. Sebastian leverages his deep technical capabilities effortlessly, as he brings to bear a deep humanistic view of design. He has also risen to challenges and gone extreme. When he brought the idea to Larry Page, he said it might take 10 years, and Larry suggested he do it in three. Eighteen months later, the prototype was ready. Online education had already been around, but MOOCs increased scale and technical sophistication by leaps and bounds. Spend an afternoon with him, and you'll see him conduct all kinds of thought experiments—it seems to be always about seeing the possibilities. Once a big idea emerges, that's when his engineering DNA kicks in and there comes the big leap![1]

You may have had your jolt already, or you may be reading this knowing that it pays to be prepared. Before you make the leap, let's make sure to consider some of the practical considerations to addressing your personal jolts, and let's make sure you have a checklist of preparations handy.

Let's start by considering a few circumstances when you should start considering proactively assembling your career catapult.

Sometimes the signs are blazing out like a big neon sign. I tend to know when change is afoot when I start getting invitations to connect on LinkedIn from multiple people in a company that is clearly starting to lay people off and people are scrambling to connect with potential career boosters and influencers. You may see such signs in your company if it has started wave after wave of layoffs, or the technology you have worked with for years is rapidly being sunset across the industry. I spent a chunk of my life in a company I loved, but as I started watching some of the smartest strategists no longer having a spot in the company, it was obvious that the future was about operational priorities. My particular focus on innovation and organizational change was going to be inevitably questioned. I knew I would need to move on. I still love the company and products, though!

There may be situations where you can see your own role seeming to erode when the decisions you used to make are now being made by others and when you no longer appear to belong or matter. Or, like in the previous example, maybe your friends and colleagues are proactively leaving. Even if you are feeling secure, consider whether there may be signs that your skill set or mind-set is going out of fashion. These are difficult signs to ignore.

Others are more subtle. You get a sense that you're getting passed over, whether it's a promotion that goes to another type of colleague altogether or when plum projects get passed on to other "high potentials." You feel like the way you evaluate work and the environment is in stark contrast to the way your company and industry does; for example, the accountant who realized that the pure bottom-line orientation of the banking industry was just not enough for him.

Then there are the deeply personal signs. That's when it's been years since you've had a good night's sleep on a Sunday night, when you just can't handle going in on Monday morning. On the other end of the spectrum, you may be looking at your mid-30s, and realizing that you are just too comfortable. You are just not challenged and your learning curve has flattened. You could do your boss's job, but you don't see any sign of getting there any time soon. Worse, you are looking over the wall into other companies and seeing people with your experience and tenure learning and being stretched every day. You have a safe job and you're on auto-pilot. How do you up the ante and push yourself forward?

This last situation is a tough one to shake up. How do you explain to friends and family that you're starting to pull the catapult rubber band because you're too comfortable? Just say it like it is: "I know I can do more."

Then there is that day you wake up and realize you like very little about your situation: the goals you have to deliver on, your team, your boss, and the company's vision. In fact, it's easier when you actually dislike something. What if you are just indifferent or not inspired? I knew I was done in a banking job the day I looked up from work as one of my internal clients came in and asked me, "So, Roopa, how do you feel about the job?" and I said, "Hey, it's a job."

Make sure to test these strategies to ensure that you are not acting on what is basically a short-term blockage.

If you're getting passed over, you can check to see that it's not just some practical issue. Do you have specific certifications you can take to continue being attractive to your organization? Have you taken the opportunity to talk to senior influencers to show that you are ready, willing, and able?

Checkpoint: Take the Long View

Make sure you're running toward something, rather than just running away from something. A career catapult is most effective and inspired when you're not just battling a negative experience and weighed down by baggage. In addition, making a change happen is hard work and requires commitment. If you're responding to a temporary issue or an easily solvable situation, you may lose steam along the way. The best change efforts are built on a bedrock of conviction.

Here are some quick tests to make sure that you are not reacting to solvable issues:

- Is this about money?
  - Try this mind game. What would happen if the accounting department or your boss walked in right now and told you that you were going to make 10 percent more starting today? Would you be excited enough

to recommit to the job? If the answer is yes, then start figuring out how to ask for a raise constructively and with good data about your contributions to the business.

- Could a certification or specific skill make you more attractive in your current situation or add to your promotion-readiness?
  - Take out a note pad and start listing the skills and certification. Now figure out how you will access some of these online, what training the company provides, and where can you get on-the-job training and experience with these skills. This may be a time to hunker down for now and add to your skill-set, rather than catapulting out of there.
- Is this about one specific project or set of projects?
  - Even if it looks like there's no end in sight, can you either hand the project off or rationally plan for the end of the project?

- Is this about just one or a small set of colleagues or is it just feeling like a bad fit?
  - Might you be able to find another spot in the company that would work better? Better yet, can you find other roles for these people?
- Is this about leaders who don't know how ambitious you are?
  - Women have this issue a lot. You aren't getting feedback and your learning curve has flattened. You know you should be adding to your skills—technical, management, or both. Be proactive; ask for new projects, share your aspirations, find mentors and guides inside the company, and sign up for training programs.

Now that you've done that test, does it still feel like it's more long-term and deeper than the test indicates? If so, then great—it's time to catapult! Once you have tested and established that this is not just a short-term, addressable issue, you need to get going.

You've followed the book. You're inspired, you have a sense of what your new spaces might be, and you've been prototyping and going extreme. Now what?

In the innovation economy, it's no longer a matter of sending out resumes as soon as you decide you are ready to make a move; rather, it's about building momentum with time so that the momentum is there to support them as you walk right into the next opportunity. That's a different kind of marketing and it is ongoing. Moreover, it's not just about writing a resume, but about telling one's story and ensuring that the right people hear it. The assets someone brings to the task are the narrative of their experience and abilities, their Rolodex, social media, and even their social life. You'll need to keep them unlocked and ready to go so that they are naturally primed for the next change when and as it emerges.

Let's discuss how you will craft your story so it is ready to be projected when needed. Let's also discuss how to get it out there in the right way to the right audiences with every jolt you initiate.

What we'll discuss is not just for the initial jump. It's also for when you land in this new reality you have made for yourself.

Michael Watkins first wrote about successfully transitioning into a new job in *The First 90 Days* in 2003.[2] His research suggests a systematic approach to the early days of being in a job. In essence, you have 90 days to prove you are an asset to the company upon entering a new job. Given that constraint, time is of the essence. Recognize the impact of a leader's arrival, and make sure you plan for the change. Communicate and promote when you achieve the clear change goals you set for those 90 days and beyond. The book is a bestseller for many reasons, including the encyclopedic nature of the game plan Watkins lays out.

So what do the social and digital realms add to that rich book? Here are a few quick insights.

Tell Your Story Yourself

Whether you proactively moved from your last situation, crafted your new start-up yourself, or were asked to leave, success lies in taking control of the story. Don't fabricate; lay out the facts and then do the right thing by the people around you and clarify the decisions you made and outcomes you were working toward. Tell the story proactively and the authenticity will come through.

Every element of your career path is part of your overall brand story line. Your decisions were made in a context, and helping others understand that context is the best way to underscore your values.

As you catapult, remember that in many ways you are going to be in sales mode. Rather than a product or service, you're selling the idea of you. Your future investor, clients, and bosses aren't buying from a big corporate brand; they need to get a sense of you: what you represent, your values, and your beliefs. They want to know that they can do business with you. Making sure you represent that story and voice on all your online spaces can be the difference between excellence and confusion.

As in all cases, it's about the what, but also the how.

Just like in real life, active networking is a key strategy to building a core personal and business brand. It does mean stretching yourself, as in real life, to take action and in some cases to push yourself into taking that extra step.

There are, among us, the gregarious, externally oriented folks who are energized by the prospect of meeting new people and engaging with old contacts. For those of us who may be a little uncomfortable with networking, you may find yourself better motivated by giving yourself specific goals to that networking effort.

Consider all your online platforms—your Website, blog, LinkedIn, Instagram, Facebook, and Twitter accounts—as tools for appropriate networking. In each case, you set forth a personable and engaging personality, listen to those who engage with you on each platform, and respond effectively. By the way, you don't have to do all of them! Find the ones that make the most sense for your industry, your workflow, and your life flow.

What does it mean to establish and display a consistent and authentic online personality?

It starts with knowing what you would like to stand for. In my case, as I developed my online brand, I set out to be thoughtful about innovation, leadership, strategy, and business culture. As a coach, my effort is also to help my clients get to the answer themselves, not just telling them the answer. My consulting hinges on having a nuanced understanding of all of these organizational drivers. In addition, my real-life and online personality melds; my intent is to be helpful and thoughtful. So I work to keep my online voice personified by asking a thoughtful question about interesting phenomena I see or sharing helpful articles and always acknowledging who first brought it to my attention. Spend some time on my blog or Twitter feed and you'll see what I mean.

Also recognize that this effort will take some time and discipline. In Sree Sreenivasan's case, this means a strategic use of a series of tools and taking the time to craft his tweets. Getting 140 characters to truly represent your best thinking is not a trivial task. If you can, try and schedule a set time on your calendar, maybe even a 30-minute block first thing in the morning, to set up a Hootsuite (or Buffer) feed that will automatically post throughout the day, setting up your insights to hit your different networks at appropriate times during the work day.

Experiment and take chances; there are many free platforms out there for you. Find out where the right customer groups and eyeballs live for your specific business. For example, if yours is a fun product that is publicly used, maybe an Instagram and Pinterest feed that shows your product being used in fun and funky ways is for you. If it's about thought leadership, marshal the resources of LinkedIn and join the right groups where your thinking will be seen and recognized for its expertise. Watch the take-up of your work and then refine your use of the platform to put your best personality and assets forward.

Now take that big next step: let your physical and virtual worlds collide. Find online those people you meet in routine and professional events. Engage with them, watch them, and be supportive of them. Then draw the insights you see online into real life.

Always remember, online platforms are not just broadcast platforms, they are listening posts. Be expansive; listen to the topics that charge you up and that are relevant. Sree recommends obsessing about "followees" as much as followers, because they will serve up extremely rare nuggets of information. In the end, it's not who follows you on social media that matters—it's who follows who follows you. Find and connect with influencers in your field.

Here are some concrete steps for you to take:

- Identify your brand drivers: what do you do and what do you want to stand for?

- Recognize your voice: be clear on how you want to sound online. Is it thoughtful, irreverent, provocative, or helpful? It doesn't matter which; it should just be authentic to you or what you think your brand would be.
- Be clear on your goal: are you selling or influencing? Both are important, but branding is about the latter, not the former.
- Experiment with platforms: test platforms on a trial basis to see what suits your target customers and influencers.
- Choose a few paid tools that can make your work easier, including Hootsuite and SocialFlow (depending on your budget).
- Remember it's about a suite of platforms. Things change online, and you shouldn't be dependent on one platform. More importantly, each platform has its strengths, so make sure to use them well.
- Have fun. See Sree's social media success formula that can guide you along as well.

@Sree's Social Media Success Formula

Your tweets, Facebook postings, etc. should have as many of these attributes as possible:

- ➤ Helpful
- ➤ Useful
- ➤ Timely
- ➤ Informative
- ➤ Relevant
- ➤ Practical
- ➤ Actionable
- ➤ Generous
- ➤ Credible
- ➤ Brief
- ➤ Entertaining
- ➤ Fun and occasionally funny!

Design Your Next Role

There are certainly jobs out there that stick to the tried-and-true format, such as HR manager, for example. But in reality, the *kind* of HR manager you are depends on how you visualize the goals. You could take the conventional approach and stick to the current processes *or* you can be someone who unleashes the power of social media and digital data to drive your people's strategy. It's a rare HR team and company that truly mine leadership and management metrics. Companies have made a science of reviewing revenue and cost of goods. SAP (systems, applications, products) and various ERP (enterprise resource planning) systems can tell you exactly how many widgets and man hours go into the last car, headphone, or jar of grape jelly produced. How about the quality of management that went into crafting those products and services? A plethora of information exists on what makes for good management and great teams.

It's often not too much of a stretch to identify the exemplary employees and managers in an organization, but rarely do we take a data-focused approach to understanding and using those insights. We're good about giving our 11-year-olds a sense of where they stand against their peers in their proficiency at various subjects, as well as tracking key input metrics like class participation. Isn't it only fair that we provide that kind of transparency to managers in our organizations, given how much of an impact they have on the bottom line? We've known the key drivers for a while. For example, in the 1998 study of Sears by Rucci, Qirn, and Quinn, they found that "when employee satisfaction improved by 5 percent, customer satisfaction improved by 1.3 percent, which led to a .05 percent improvement in revenue." At $50 billion in annual revenue for Sears at that time, that came to an extra $250 million in sales.[3] A 2014 study by James Harter and Randall Beck has shown that four people practices related to managers—selecting managers who are engagement oriented, the manager's ability to hire for skills, feedback to their teams on strengths, and interest in people management—can drive up to a 59 percent increase in revenue for the team, ergo the company.[4]

What if you're the HR person who can lay out how managers with high retention rates and who promoted diversity also have higher revenue and productivity metrics? There's a lot of money at stake here. Wouldn't it be useful for each employee to know where they stand against these high impact folks? Would you be changing the paradigm of development? Better yet, would you be setting yourself up to catapult further and faster?

Remember to Name It Yourself

People like to put people in neat boxes. It's your job to redefine and rename your box. Make sure that you start describing your work and what you do in a way that makes it clear that you're not the "plain vanilla" version. The HR person who does what I just described shouldn't be called an HR generalist; rather, he or she is an HR strategist, a people management officer, or the head of people and talent.

Don't get jingoistic. It's not about being cute or cutesy. It's about helping people get beyond the norm. As businesses and technologies collide, jobs and roles are evolving faster than the job board will ever acknowledge. When I was in school, there was no such thing as a chief innovation officer or even an innovation program outside of R&D. Now, most self-respecting companies have innovation teams, continuous innovation teams, UI/UX groups, and so on. As you reflect on how you can drive impact, define it in ways that explain you and the outcomes you deliver.

Don't just toss it out there; contextualize it as well. If you're an innovation leader, explain how your goal is to drive product innovation, partnerships, or business-model changes. If you are about social engagement, ensure you connect it to the business outcomes you can drive.

My favorite title came about when Vasumathi Soundararajan left Oscar De La Renta to create her men's designer underwear start-up, Ken Wroy. She launched a whole new title as well—she is the Chief Underwearist!

What titles do I hope to see going forward? How about virtual reality communications lead, head of collaborative insights (for when sensors provide companies insights that they can collaborate across industries), or chief engagement officer for when social media, marketing, real-time information exchange, and sales truly collide.

Do the Math

One of the very practical steps you should take is to set out your financial plan. Whether you're looking at changing jobs, making a jump, going back into retraining, or becoming an entrepreneur, you should go into that catapult fully armed with knowledge. You're looking at exciting new opportunities, but work with a financial professional or work with your pen and notepad to make sure you know the following:

- Will you be going small to go big? In other words, will you need to plan for a pay cut as you make this change?

- Do you have enough put away to weather a period of transition? Depending on the extent of change, making sure you have a financial cushion of between six to 18 months of expenses may make sense.
- If you don't have that financial cushion, do you have a support network that can help?
- What additional expenses do you see in the immediate horizon? For example, what are the coaching, new training, or transport costs (if you move to a different geography)?
- Will you need to relocate? Does that mean selling a home?
- What kind of financial disruption is the family going to have to plan for?

Make sure you know the logistical impact of your next few steps. Don't be deterred; just be prepared.

I remember first developing my business plan for my own consulting practice in 2008. I did my research, checked in on those I saw as my ideal clients (their feedback helped me frame my offerings), and built out my strengths and gaps. In addition, I kept doing the math and it was only by 2011 that I began to feel more confident about my ability to make the big leap. I needed to make sure we'd be able to pay the mortgage and fund college funds. Having a financial plan helped me take the plunge as well as helped me get the family aligned.

Make the Jump

Remember, you will never ever be fully prepared for all the excitement that comes with a career catapult.

Take the case of the founder of Ken Wroy, Vasumathi Soundararajan, the "Chief Underwearist" I mentioned before. In Vasumathi's case, the jump to developing her own start-up was propelled by a series of events that stretched the catapult band. She had always been artistic and loved crafting things with her own hands, and coming out of school she had reached out to her network to see what the career opportunities for someone in design would be. However, she was from a family of academicians and engineers, and business seemed like a bridge too far. The one person who had graduated from the National Institute of Design, her bona fide "cool older friend," didn't do much to help her visualize a strong future possibility. As a result, rather than take on her first love, she chose to work in a space she felt capable: journalism.

A few years later, she found herself working in a fabulous TV producer role, and yes, somehow uninspired by the career paths opening up before her. She found a way to insert her passion for the cool and pop culture into journalism, writing, and producing provocative pieces on urban fashion, music, and film. It was the time of reality shows and quizzes, and although it was fabulous entertainment, she felt empty.

Vasumathi was sure there were richer pastures out there and decided to go extreme. New York was it and she proceeded to design her portfolio. It took her two tries, and she landed at the Fashion Institute of Technology, where she went extreme again. Although she could have managed with 12 credits each semester, she packed in 21 credits each time. "Paisa wasool," she laughs, the Indian slang for ROI (return on investment), because foreign students paid a flat fee. Her design instinct always drew her to menswear, and she took the extra menswear courses offered on weekends and also got couture certificates that taught her hand embroidery techniques that are getting lost.

Vasumathi also had a moment of incredible serendipity. She found her muse in Tim, who would eventually become her husband. She met this young French scholar at the Alliance Francaise in Bangalore, and his openness to moving anywhere in the world was a key element of her evolution. As she confronted the emptiness of her journalism career, she engaged more fully with her past passion—design. Tim was a helpful sounding board. More importantly, as she worked in a series of unpaid internships that are typical of the design world, she had a partner in crime. Here was someone who rolled with her musings about the straight guys' inability to enjoy shopping. Tim would inspire her in many ways, including letting her scrutinize his dreary wardrobe, refreshing it, and having him chat with his network of friends to test her emerging ideas. Finally, although Vasumathi was always intrigued by the business model of small vendors around her—the sandwich stand, the house maid—she'd been a little intimidated by the math. In Tim, she found a complementary set of skills.

Vasumathi went extreme in a different way—she went small. Rather than attack the whole menswear stage, she was intrigued by her girlfriends who would giggle about all the natty Wall Street men they dated, who wore surprisingly boring underwear. She decided to go small, focusing on men's underwear. She made her first prototypes by hand, testing on focus groups and retail stores. She was warmly received and she knew she held the key to real success in her hand.

Once she had her overall line set up, and her production partners in Colombia, she jumped. Leaving the ateliers of Oscar De La Renta and Catherine Maladrino was easy, not only because she had found her muse and passion, but also because she knew clearly that the high-end couture of the designer was not her thing. They did give her the eye and the sense of the business dynamics, and she built on them to craft her own masterpiece: Ken Wroy.

Vasumathi talks about how she ends each day by totally disconnecting from any industry news or business talk. She prefers connecting to things that intrigue her and help her connect to things beyond her, connecting to things bigger than her, as she frames it. One of her favorites is to watch animal documentaries, which helped her design one of her best-selling pieces. Her Giraffe underwear has mirrored giraffes, an homage to Alexander McQueen, the master designer she adores. The giraffes create an illusion of the man's bottom being rounder and bigger. She revels in her craft, and it was fun to hear her discuss the fun and frankly sexual connotations of the giraffe in a professional context. Here was someone having fun at work!

———————

It's true that the jump won't be easy. You will face unfamiliar terrain: responsibilities you didn't expect, people who talk a different idiom, lingo and jargon that you'll be Googling discretely on your smartphone, and technologies that aren't quite what you expect!

This doesn't mean that you wait to get to perfection. Your best bet is to embrace the uncertainty and let the catapult snap.

- Remember the value you bring to the table: your skills, capabilities, and the black holes you will avoid.

- Use your existing network to prepare for the change, but also continue to authentically build a strong network that will support you through the transition.

- Disrupt yourself constantly. Remember, like many start-ups, you may need to pivot even when you are in a new role or have your new entrepreneurial plan going. You may not do it perfectly, but you're going to impress yourself and those around you a lot more than if you had refused to try the move and learn as you went along.

- Manage yourself. Needless to say, you're going to feel stressed and that's normal. But if you relentlessly pursue the end goal (that is, finally figuring out what in the world you're supposed to be doing and how to do it) with confidence and initiative, you'll make it out of the deep end and probably sooner than you think.

Rinse and Repeat

The catapult may sound like it's one-and-done. Not so. Remember, this is really about building a mindset of continuous learning. Keep a watch out for the skills to beef up or acquire, and for the people or institutions that can help you jolt your career to the next level. Most importantly, keep stalking the trends. That shift never stops, so make it a game that you enjoy playing and you'll be doing well.

And then it's about keeping an eye out for the next big leap—it's about going extreme!

AFTERWORD

The impetus for my writing this book came from the multiple discussions I had with colleagues who struggled with the constraints of their roles, and with the prospect of being "stuck," as well as my coaching sessions with clients who felt left behind after years of contributing to the goals of corporations. It is also an homage to the intrepid entrepreneurs and investors who wake up every morning and put their effort and money where their mouth is.

All take different paths, but all are inspired by our own personal jolts and opportunities. It's always an interesting ride. Jolts stop us in our tracks but also can provide the momentum to shift to new paths to success. I hope you will find this book helpful in your own pathway to success.

My greatest wish is that you will truly engage with the exercises described in this book. Please go to *www.TheCareerCatapult.com* and click on the "Worksheets" button on the homepage. Enter "MyCatapult" and access all the worksheets. Welcome to your career catapult!

CHAPTER NOTES

Chapter 2

1. Daniel Pink, *Drive: The Surprising Truth About What Motivates Us* (New York: Riverhead Books, 2011). Kindle edition, 1815. Referring to the research done by Adam Grant.

2. For example, Ola Svenson writes in the Swedish psychology journal *Acta Psychologica* that a whopping 93 percent of Americans consider themselves above average drivers, whereas only 69 percent of Swedes think so. See: http://sciencedirect.com/science/article/pii/0001691881900056.

3. Arthur Quiller-Couch (ed.) *The Oxford Book of English Verse, 1250–1900* (Oxford: Clarendon, 1919).

4. Mihály Csíkszentmihályi, *Flow: The Psychology of Optimal Experience* (New York: Harper & Row, 1990).

5. George Day, "Is It Real? Can We Win? Is It Worth Doing?: Managing Risk and Reward in an Innovation Portfolio," *Harvard Business Review*, December, 2007. https://hbr.org/2007/12/is-it-real-can-we-win-is-it-worth-doing-managing-risk-and-reward-in-an-innovation-portfolio.

6. E.A. Maguire, K. Woollett, and H.J. Spiers, *London Taxi Drivers and Bus Drivers: A Structural MRI and Neuropsychological Analysis.* Abstract, 2006, https://ncbi.nlm.nih.gov/pubmed/17024677.

Chapter 3

1. "$24.5 Billion in Revenue Left on the Table by U.S. Retailers and Financial Services Last Year Due to Poor Mobile User Experience," Jumio.com, August 2015,

https://jumio.com/2015/08/24-5-billion
-in-revenue-left-on-the-table-by-mobile
-businesses-and-financial-services-last-year
-due-to-poor-user-experience/.

2. Jack Neff, "Revlon Counts on 'Selling
   Hope' to Make Up for Its Small Size,"
   Advertising Age, September 2012, http://
   adage.com/article/cmo-interviews/revlon
   -counts-selling-hope-make-size/236961/.

3. "Building for the next moment," May 5,
   2015, Google internal data published on
   Google Inside AdWords.

4. Adam Lella and Andrew Lipsman, "2016
   U.S. Cross-Platform Future in Focus,"
   ComScore.com, March 2016, www
   .comscore.com/Insights/Presentations
   -and-Whitepapers/2016/2016-US-Cross
   -Platform-Future-in-Focus.

Chapter 5

1. "Child Rights and You," accessed
   December 16, 2016, https://en.wikipedia
   .org/wiki/Child_Rights_and_You.

Chapter 6

1. Jeff Chu, "Sree Sreenivasan: For liberating the museum from its physical walls," *Fast Company*, May 2015, www.fastcompany .com/3043932/most-creative-people-2015 /sree-sreenivasan.

2. Jenni Avins, "The Met ousted a top executive, so he used Facebook to show the world how to do unemployment right," *Quartz*, June 2016, http://qz.com/711943 /sree-sreenivasan-how-to-spin-getting -fired-from-your-high-profile-job-into-a -delightful-digital-campaign/.

3. C.K. Prahalad and Richard Bettis, "The Dominant Logic: A New Linkage Between Diversity and Performance," *Strategic Management Journal* 7(6):485–501, November 1986, https://researchgate.net /profile/Richard_Bettis/publication /230234545_The_Dominant_Logic_A _New_Linkage_Between_Diversity_and _Performance/links/5659c37108ae1ef 9297fb294.pdf.

4. "Imposter syndrome," accessed December 18, 2016, https://en.wikipedia.org/wiki /Impostor_syndrome.

Chapter 7

1. Max Chafkin, "Udacity's Sebastian Thrun, Godfather of Free Online Education, Changes Course," *Fast Company*, November 2013, https://fastcompany.com/3021473 /udacity-sebastian-thrun-uphill-climb.

2. Michael Watkins, *The First 90 Days: Critical Success Strategies for New Leaders at All Levels* (Boston, Mass.: Harvard Business School Press, 2003).

3. Jack Zenger and Joseph Folkman, "How Damaging Is a Bad Boss, Exactly?" *Harvard Business Review*, July 2012, https://hbr.org /2012/07/how-damaging-is-a-bad-boss-exa.

4. James Harter and Randall Beck, "New Research: How Four Talent Practices Add Up to Big Revenue Gains," *Harvard Business Review*, May 2014, https://hbr .org/2014/05/how-four-talent-practices -add-up-to-big-revenue-gains.

INDEX